Brick

A Perch of Birds (1880) by Hector Giacomelli

Brick

a literary journal

number 105

summer 2020

PUBLISHER: Laurie D. Graham
EDITORS: Dionne Brand, David Chariandy,
Laurie D. Graham, Michael Helm, Liz Johnston,
Martha Sharpe, Rebecca Silver Slayter, Madeleine Thien
MANAGING EDITOR: Allison LaSorda
ASSISTANT EDITOR & CIRCULATION MANAGER: Sarah Melton
CONTRIBUTING EDITORS: Teju Cole, Robert Hass,
Anne McLean, Tara Quinn
ART DIRECTOR: Mark Byk
READERS: Neve Dickson, Marcia Walker, Orly Zebak,
Jack Donnelly, Rachel Gerry
ORIGINAL DESIGN: Gordon Robertson, Rick/Simon
LOGOS: David Bolduc
COPY EDITOR: Heather Sangster
WEBSITE DESIGN: Mark Byk with Matthew McKinnon
FOUNDERS: Stan Dragland & Jean McKay

*Works of art are of an infinite loneliness and with
nothing to be so little reached as with criticism.
Only love can grasp and hold and fairly judge them.*
— Rainer Maria Rilke

ISSN 0382-8565, ISBN 978-1-928166-12-2
Publications Mail Agreement No. 40042720
Return undeliverable Canadian addresses to

BRICK
Box 609, Stn P
Toronto, Ontario M5S 2Y4
Canada

We gratefully acknowledge the support of the Canada
Council for the Arts and the Ontario Arts Council.

BRICK accepts unsolicited manuscripts of non-fiction *only*.
Please submit through Submittable or mail submissions to

BRICK
Box 609, Stn P
Toronto, Ontario M5S 2Y4
Canada

Subscribe online at BRICKMAG.COM

From time to time we make our subscriber list available
to similar-minded magazines or arts organizations.
To be excluded from these mailings, please email us at
INFO@BRICKMAG.COM or write to us.

BRICK is published twice yearly by Cypress Avenue Inc.
and is printed and bound in Canada by L'Empreinte.
Distributed in Canada by Magazines Canada, in the
United States by ANC, and overseas by Central Books.

In This Issue

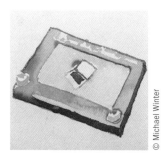

© Michael Winter

The photograph on our front cover is Pink Matters © *2017 Serge Najjar. The photographs on our inside front and back covers are* Echoes *and* Gates to Nowhere © *2018 & 2019, Serge Najjar.*

This is the way we make the past. This is the way I will make it here. Listening for hooves. Glimpsing the red hat which was never there in the first place. Giving eyesight and evidence to a woman we never knew and cannot now recover. And for all our violations, the past waits for us.

— Eavan Boland

Cy Twombly, *Fifty Days at Iliam:*
Shield of Achilles (1978)

Cy Twombly, *Fifty Days at Iliam: The Fire that Consumes All Before it* (1978)
© CY TWOMBLY FOUNDATION

Cy Twombly, *Fifty Days at Iliam:*
Ilians in Battle (1978)
© CY TWOMBLY FOUNDATION

Studies for Excursus

DEAN RADER

Cy Twombly,
Fifty Days at Iliam *(1978)*

And it goes like this:
And it goes into the into.
And it goes out on a horse.
And it goes like victory,

                    says The Into.

So many have galloped,

                  barebacked, into themselves.
So many have taken both the blue pill and the red pill.
So many are anvil-hearted,

                hammer-hearted.
So many removed their arms so their hands could not be nailed,

                      thousands.

Wir die Deutschen

LINA MERUANE

Translated from the Spanish by Andrea Rosenberg

checkpoints

We came from different countries and a variety of disciplines; our bodies ran the gamut. An out-spoken Greek activist. A young, white Egyptian filmmaker. Two Senegalese rappers, one slimmer and quieter and darker than the other. A professor of Indian art and her Indian-via-California husband, also a university professor. A German philosopher with tousled red hair. The Chilestinian writer—me—and the actual Palestinians: the curator who'd summoned all of us from Berlin, the historian who'd returned from Chicago and was teaching at a local university on an expired visa, the feminist anthropologist from Jerusalem. A photographer with a thick salt-and-pepper beard and a journalist only recently released from an Israeli prison. And although we weren't a large group, we were occasionally joined by experts who could explain the most incomprehensible political events. We had come together to share a week of rising at dawn in a little hotel in Ramallah, seven days of overeating and excess coffee, of chain-smoking cigarettes just so we foreigners could tolerate the difficult life that Palestinians endure every day. We would be piling into a brightly coloured minibus for our outings, avoiding the exclusive Israeli highways and using instead the Palestinian roads periodically interrupted by fixed and mobile checkpoints that were not crossings, as the Israelis claimed, but points of control, of capture, of interrogation, of enervating waits. We would stop at these mahsoms, show our passports, and continue along dirt roads; we would visit orchards, walls, wails, contested mosques, beehives amid rubble, houses in ruins, occupied houses, wastelands, barriers dividing towns and families, mahsoms that were certainly not *crossings* since it was no simple thing to move through them, the rows of semi-detached houses in the settlements, the red-roofed Israeli neighbourhoods, mahsoms; we would see walls papered over with the faces of child martyrs, children who'd been murdered by soldiers in a scuffle or murdered just because, for being there and being Palestinian, there, now, in fenced-off or long-closed markets, among Arab theatres and dabke schools and stores selling natural soap and spices in burlap sacks, cultural centres built by hand, bulldozed houses, caves full of bats, walls, walls, hotels, checkpoints, security cameras, bus stations, checkpoints watchtowers checkpoints.

matter of time

Time has been wrested from them, along with so many other things. Time is the thing that's denied to Palestinians in the hundreds of checkpoints where they are deliberately detained. Their identities demanded. Their papers examined and checked against other papers, other names, other faces. They are forced to wait as many minutes hours days months as the soldiers wish and are never told why or how long it will be. A wedding, a baptism, a birthday party: those can wait. A funeral, a heart attack. It can wait. The cancer treatment that isn't available in the occupied territories. It will have to wait, without knowing how long. Without knowing what lies ahead. Part of the violence lies in that arbitrariness, that not knowing what the protocol is or if a protocol even exists. Not being able to plan the present, not being able to think

about the future. Control over time is a rifle loaded with humiliation. But Palestinians have built a kind of armour against that violence. Knowing that the soldiers are seeking their impatience and desperation, they've developed counterattack strategies. The Palestinian photographer, slowly stroking his beard, explains it to me as we wait at one of the checkpoints for soldiers to review our papers. We Palestinians have learned to relish extreme slowness, he says, his black eyes glinting in the sunlight. If they tell us to move, we comply, only very slowly; if they order us to stop, we allow our bodies to go heavy while our minds disconnect; we drag our tongues during interrogations, rummage around for our papers for a long time, claiming that we can't find them. We are no longer troubled by impatience. Immediacy has no appeal. Speed: the swiftness that characterizes destructive capitalism. We simply space out, he says; Safn-in! he says; and I'm surprised to discover that this idiom, literally "to be on the moon," appears in so many languages, that in so many places, among so many unarmed people, inhabiting a parallel reality means not to be excluded but to endure. Bi shu safin? To stare off into the distance. Leish safin fiyyi? Paradoxical though it may sound, the Palestinian photographer continues, if we waste time or get lost in time, the soldiers can no longer wield time against us. They can't use something to harm us if we refuse to care about it. And we strike back at the soldiers by making them waste the very time they try in vain to snatch from us.

a teutonic chorus

At a snail's pace, we are passing signs that announce settlements with Hebrew names and rarely the names of Palestinian towns; if the driver weren't a local, we would remain trapped in the ongoing limbo of the checkpoints. Our driver, unfazed, keeps his window open in case a soldier appears and motions for him to stop or another soldier tries to peer in through that hatch. The soldiers are always young—they look like students pursuing a useless degree or inexperienced actors. The door to the minibus slides open like a stage curtain and one of them climbs in, his boots banging on the step, and brandishing his rifle, yells something in Hebrew. Nobody understands. Nobody responds. The driver mutters to the soldier that we're foreigners, so the young man clears his throat, tunes his vocal cords, and shouts again in English, our bus's lingua franca: Where are you from? He addresses us as a group, but each of our passports contains a different answer, and the Palestinians, who do not have them at all, are hidden in the back. Where are you from?! he repeats impatiently, addressing the German philosopher in the front row. Germany, Germany responds, his hair redder and more tousled than ever, but only Greece and I, also in the front row, across the aisle, hear his meek response. Where?! the soldier roars, trying to impose his authority, but Germany is twice his age and size and now he raises a fearsome and booming Teutonic voice and says his homeland's name again, Gerrrmany, and the name of his city, Berlin, now freed from siege and the infamous wall that Israel has seen fit to replicate in these lands. Berrrlin, he clarifies, in case the soldier is unfamiliar with the name of the country Germany. The soldier stands silent with his hand outstretched, demanding the passport, and as he examines it he glances toward the rearmost seats, and maybe he's

nearsighted because he does not spot the Palestinian faces crowded in the farthest reaches of the bus. He notices only the straight, almost white hair of a Greek who's gone albino with fright, our Greece, who's huddled in her seat. Are we all *Germans*? The soldier raises his voice as his myopic eyes glide over us, and from us rises a resounding German *Yes*, an African and Indian and Palestinian *Yes!*, plus a *Jaaaa!* that probably comes from Egypt, who has a German surname and a German passport, as well as a face suffused with Germanness. *We are all Germans!*

karneval

As soon as the door closes, Greece starts shouting, her voice mocking, Germany! Germany!, rolling the *r*'s in her Hellenic mouth. Chile howls an ironic Chili!, although nobody seems to get the irony, nobody seems to know that the *e* that ends Chile does not sound like an *i*, it's not a spicy land, just an insignificant country shaped like a hot pepper. Egypt raises his German arms as if he's just kicked the ball into the enemy's goal; he throws his head back. And the Senegalese trill in unison, We the Germans, and the Indian couple joins in the chorus of booming, uproarious Palestinian laughter full of memorable vowels. In that revelry of bared gums and accents, our German philosopher sits up straight. Realizing that we aren't actually laughing, but instead casting off our fear through our mouths, he joins in with his own Saxon chortle of victory. Even so, we know without saying it, without hinting at it, without venturing regret, that our infraction has been completely misguided. We have donned the armour of a nation that is at the heart of the conflict. We have used its name as a talisman. We have invoked Germany, which is still paying reparations to the state of Israel for brutal abuses committed many decades earlier, while overlooking the abuses the Israelis are committing against the Palestinians in the present. It was absolutely necessary that nobody ever forget the theft and expropriation and relentless extermination of millions of German and European Jews and a horrifying number of Roma, gays, and the mentally ill, and children who were cognitively impaired or supposedly inferior, and anyone else who did not comport with the vaunted notions of Aryan supremacy. And because it was necessary never to forget, never to forget it in order never to repeat it, the Germans decided to educate the populace against antisemitism and to pay economic reparations at the end of that cruel war they fortunately lost. But they continue to pay and flagellate themselves without ever demanding, not even seventy years after Israel's creation, that the Israelis stop criminalizing and imprisoning thousands of Palestinians—young, old, children healthy and sick alike, women veiled or uncovered—that they stop demolishing Palestinian houses, destroying their neighbourhoods, multiplying the illegal settlements on Palestinian lands that were supposed to be protected by an international law that no nation seemed to respect. Not even Germany. Because only now, seventy years on, has Germany

ventured to express, via its powerful chancellor, some timid disagreement with the violence perpetrated by Israel against its Palestinian minority and against the Palestinian majority of the territories it occupies. A territory that we, die Deutschen, are now occupying under the cover of Germany's name. We will have to be strategic, to keep using our adopted German status to secure safe passage. We know that saying Palestine would have been a terrible idea and saying Chile—or chili!—a bad idea, since Chile, too, is a land of Palestinians. Saying Egypt or Senegal or India would have been asking them to check our passports and interrogate our minds and souls. Even Greece, a member of the European Union, isn't European enough because Greece, Greece whispers, her face puffy, still laughing but a little upset, is only a crossroads, a place between cultures. But Greece is Europe, I whisper, not wishing to contradict her, since as a Greek she'd know better than I. But she presses her lips together resentfully and, narrowing her eyes, says that even though Greece is the cradle of Western civilization and its philosophers invented the democracy that nobody in the West has ever truly implemented, northern Europeans consider it to be an impoverished nation clinging to Europe from the south. A failed state, she says, now downcast and brow-furrowed. And putting her voice next to my ear, she murmurs that especially the Germans consider it a Mediterranean, practically Eastern nation. Few people know where exactly the fragile boundaries between the Near, Middle, and Far East lie, and Greece falls within the colonial outline of the Ottoman Empire. We gained our independence from the Turks in 1821, do you realize that? she asks

without asking, without expecting an answer. We gained our independence from them long before the Levant did, we were never Turks, never Arabs, never Africans, adds Greece, who, swathed in her long, pleated skirt, could pass for Dutch or Scandinavian. So stupid! she exclaims, still in my ear because she doesn't want to stir up trouble with Egypt or offend the Palestinians, who have left one empire only to fall into the claws of another. Make no mistake, Greece insists, her sigmas and omicrons, her taus pis deltas growing sombre. Let's not delude ourselves for even a minute that we can lay claim to the mask of Germanness. All this has been is the world's shortest costume party.

solutions

We would be Deutschen for a few days while on the bus. See how things went when we got off it, who we should be on land. We would immerse ourselves in all of our languages and all the translations of those languages until the curator, the historian, and the feminist anthropologist became drained from spending so much time reproducing everything that was said word by word or summing up Arabic paragraphs in succinct English sentences. Tired of interpreting, by late afternoon they made us fine-tune our ears and plunge into the Palestinians' language on our own. A test of our German intelligence. Could we break free of English, the language of diplomacy but also of espionage and war? Were we capable of reading body language and moving lips? Seeing us hopelessly lost, however, they soon took pity on us and went back to paraphrasing so we wouldn't miss out on the long lists of problems and solutions enumerated for us by our Palestinian informants. Because every time they overcame one obstacle, one unforeseen circumstance, one new restriction, further setbacks arose. For example: the group of women who needed a space to meet but didn't have one and didn't have a shekel to spare either; they went out into the streets and knocked on door after door of house after house, day after day, their heads covered by pink and brown and apricot hijabs, covered but held high; they did not beg but rather demanded shekel after shekel from their neighbours and thus managed to amass a pot of money and build a wall and then another wall, then one storey on top of another storey. With additional dollars contributed by Palestinians abroad and from a loan, the women installed a kitchen, where they intended to prepare snacks to sell and earn back what they owed. Every revolution begins with a group of women getting together to chat, one of them joked in her local Arabic, her hijab around her head; we are waging the revolution of everyday life. Another example: The old beekeeper with greying hair and his old beekeeping wife in a pink hijab, her black dress covering her down to her feet. Them and their white beehives on a hill next to the road, amid the rubble of the wall that was going up right next to them. Boxes full of stinging bees that never stung them, or so they claimed. The old woman lifted the stone securing the lid and the lid securing the hive, and the old man leaned over and reached in with his bare hands to pull out honeycomb gleaming with wax, honey, and golden bees carrying out their ceremonial work. The Indian couple snapped photos they would never share, and I, behind them, took mine as if it were possible to capture their every bee and their every word, winged, thrumming, threatened with extinction. The woman beekeeper gestured at the interior of the hive, and then at the sage and chamomile plants she grew to combat diseases because, like us, she said in her Palestinian Arabic, pointing to her chest while she paused to be translated, like us, bees contract deadly diseases and there's no need to pay for remedies besides the ones nature itself provides.

cave

Outside the birds were wheeling overhead, outside the sun was burning, but inside the cave it was darkest night, and in order to reach that night full of shrilling bats we first had to pick our way carefully down a sloping and slippery path and then toil up a steep hill. The ascent required exertion; the descent involved trying not to fall down: our bodies had become a metaphor for the enormous challenges of Palestinian territory. India had found a stick and was leaning on it as she walked. Tall Senegal and medium Senegal were propelling themselves along by rapping, Nobody can stop the waves with his hand—rapping and laughing and having us repeat the line, out of breath, as we headed toward the cave without the necessary equipment. Without the right clothing. Without the proper shoes. None of us was carrying water, not even Egypt, who was trained for the dryness of deserts. We were so thirsty we didn't waste our saliva complaining. When we reached the stone entrance, the Palestinian curator peeled a few mandarin oranges and started handing out sections of them as we sat down to rest and listen to the afternoon's lecture. Our guide was wearing sporty clothes from the torso down, while her head and shoulders were swathed in a colourful hijab and her eyes were shielded by reading glasses that did not seem to make her any nimbler. Her assistants got ready to help us; India, Senegal, Egypt, and the Palestinians stood up, giving the familiar command; and I repeated it to Greece, Yallah, yallah, but Greece seemed reluctant. She'd come with us very much against her will, in her billowy skirt and a pair of dainty red shoes, high-heeled suede ones, completely inappropriate, and she was now refusing to go down into the underground cavern. Even though we had flashlights. Even though we were following behind the cave expert yelling, Yallah. Our guide didn't insist, but she didn't stop to wait for us either. The moon-like surface was fragile, the black hole dangerous, but we were going to love it. Greece hissed that she'd rather not, but we insisted, Yallah; we pleaded, Come on, yallah? We were already there, her shoes were already ruined, we'd keep her from slipping in her ridiculous broken heels. This is an experience of resistance, the Palestinian curator remarked with sober conviction, looking around at us in case anyone else was considering quitting. But Germany was already making excuses: he was claustrophobic and might freeze up in that fathomless cave. If that happened, large and heavy as he was, how would anybody get him out of there? The curator smiled mockingly and, without responding, headed into the darkness she'd known since childhood, and we, fearing that our Deutscher Ali Baba was abandoning us, tramped after the twilight that tramped after the speleologist, who was all light. And so we moved deeper into the cave. Without looking back. Without noticing that behind us Greece was picking along in her broken, muddy shoes, and that, finding himself all alone, Germany was shaking off his claustrophobic panic and coming in as well. And behind him came Chile, carefully, Chile with her eyes fixed on the ground because she couldn't see well in the dark and was terrified of the snakes that, the cave expert claimed, could still bite you even an hour after they'd died.

brave face

We Deutschen learned more and more about the Palestinian resistance—particularly the everyday practice of plastering on a perpetual grin even when there was so much to bear. It was a brave face that the actors in the Palestinian theatre in Haifa and the young dancers training in Jerusalem's catacombs full of Israeli soldiers put on, a brave face accompanied by dark thoughts about the institutions that offered them financial assistance in exchange for the obedience and politeness of those who have nothing. They put on a brave face the way you put on a mask: behind it they scowled and bit their tongues. But there were also those who tore off the mask and refused to accept that help in exchange for censorship. They rejected the deceptive assistance of government institutions: educators who gave free workshops in the schools, young people who met in reading clubs without professors or hierarchies to discuss books such as *Liquid Modernity* by the Jewish sociologist Zygmunt Bauman. Activists who denounced the persecution of sexual minorities and prostitutes, since for many Palestinians Israel wasn't the only oppressor they despised. They weren't the only ones who wielded the stone tablets of the law.

blind faces

We would never be German even though some of us could lay claim to some sort of German identity. Maybe our red-headed philosopher, who was from there; maybe Egypt, who was only part German. But not Greece: even though she could pass for German, Greece could barely elicit European acknowledgment. Not India. Not Senegal. Not Chile, which was me, even though I was spending a year in Berlin and was learning enough survival-level Deutsch to get by on the city's streets. I wasn't about to claim German identity despite the large number of Germans in the far south of my country because that was an old story now, that tale of blond, blue-eyed settlers who'd been invited by a government minister who dreamed of "improving the race" or "bleaching the bloodline," diluting the rebellious Mapuche blood decades before the Palestinians arrived. And our Palestinian travel companions weren't German either—they weren't even authorized to enter Israel, so they didn't come with us to Haifa or on a nighttime excursion to the ghost neighbourhood of Wadi Salib. Our Palestinian curator, whose European passport enabled her to cross borders, explained that the mansions of Wadi Salib had been left vacant during the catastrophe of 1948. Their Palestinian owners had fled for a few days, believing they'd be able to return, but were never allowed to go back. The Israelis made sure of

© Allison LaSorda

it: they closed the border crossing, boarded up all the doors and windows to keep them from getting in, and Israeli law declared the homes abandoned, thereby preventing, forever after, the owners from laying claim to their property. Israel promoted and funded the aliyah of countless Jews scattered across the globe (Ashkenazi and Sephardic Jews, Maghrebi and Mizrahi Jews, the Lemba, the Beta Israel), but from the very beginning it blocked the original owners' return. Having fallen into severe disrepair, those Palestinian mansions built of yellow stone were used to take in Moroccan Jews, and the entire neighbourhood became a refugee camp. It wasn't long before the overcrowding became intolerable and the African Jews began to object to living in Wadi Salib. There were large protests. One person died. The neighbourhood was rocked by waves of violence and accusations of discrimination. The Polish Jews, who were European and white, had been given better lodgings. The African Jews demanded food, jobs, and housing and were promised they'd get it; they were moved to another neighbourhood. Wadi Salib stood vacant once more. Those houses are in ruins now. The doors torn off their hinges. The gaps that once held windows now stripped of their glass. Facades like blind faces, like masks without flesh behind them. We clambered over a wall topped with barbed wire, helping one another up, and took possession like squatters in complete darkness. We explored the house, and everybody took photos of dimly lit Palestine in the background, but I gradually fell behind, afraid, even using the flashlight on my phone, that I might trip on a stair, step in a hole, slip on the broken tiles piled up on the uneven floor. And I felt the urge to crouch down, the urge to pick up a shard of ancient tile and stick it in my purse. As if by keeping a fragment of the ruined home I could impede Palestine's imminent destruction.   B̄

The Tick

BRANDI BIRD

Grandpa yells my name and it spills on the ground like a bucket of pickerel. My name is written on the tag of a dirt dress, pulled from discards and initialled in Sharpie. I wear the histories of my cousins, and I don't want to help them clean the fish. Metal basin where my mother was bathed, where I am bathed, head checked for ticks, with matches at hand. I don't know how to swim, but I know how to run in the field before tick season dies—fat, bloody. One dug into my skin like I'm a fish being pulled to shore, anchored by its head in my head. I already have a reputation. I'm already afraid. My blood and the blood of deer before me. A history of it. A story I have told myself. Have made my mother tell me at night.

Boneyards of the Cold War

KID TEO

It's July 2018. Today is the last day of my visit to Siem Reap. Later this afternoon I have to catch my flight, and the thought of being so far away from Cambodia pains me deeply. I have failed to do so much: six years ago I moved to Asia to take a job as a professor and to be closer to Cambodia. I longed for proximity to my parents' birthplace—to see with my own eyes the landscapes of their past. I hoped to lay down some kind of record of the war they had survived, to write a book that my mother and father and brothers could see themselves in. But many things in Cambodia have taken me by surprise; it is one thing to inherit the shadows of the past, another to walk among them.

I arrive at the Cambodia War Remnant Museum, just outside of Siem Reap, about five kilometres south of the ancient ruins of Angkor Wat. In the sweltering afternoon heat, I take in the arresting sight of the fenced-in outdoor space: dozens of obsolete war machines are interspersed among the banyan and palm trees. At a glance, the rusted brown tanks and aircraft carriers merge seamlessly with the browns of the trees, soil, and pits. The remains of war are starting to be reclaimed by nature. Lifeworlds woven together. Unlike the nearby ruins of the ancient Angkor empire, an attraction that draws millions of tourists each year, this boneyard feels hidden from the world. Inside the museum, I learn that war material in Cambodia used to be scrapped for recycled metal. People salvaged what they could to make a living. I've spent time in graveyards as a child, alone in the car at night as my family members scavenged the ground for earthworms they could sell to farmers. Back then, I felt excitement at watching my parents move among the dead, but today I feel unsure of how to move through such a ghostly area.

In the compound, one caption catches my eye: "Artillery 85 mm made in China, 1946. 4.75 m length, size 85 mm, fighting power approximately 13.10 km, was used in Cambodia by Pol Pot regime (1975–1979) and was finally destroyed in 1998 at Osmach battle-field the West of Siem Reap Province." This retired artillery is a fragment of a missing picture: one of fraternity between China and Cambodia—brothers in arms, some would say. This is an image of Cambodia that most have preferred not to see, drawn instead to the iconic pictures of skulls and bones, of the sunken earth of mass graves. Many tourists have gaped at the horrors of Pol Pot's killing fields, have shaken their heads in astonishment at the sheer brutality of this regime, but few have cared to see the horrors committed before and after Pol Pot's time: the military aid that flowed from China to the Khmer Rouge, the bombs that the United States dropped on Cambodia, the refugees that were turned back at the borders.

This boneyard is a cemetery of the longue durée of imperial violence in Cambodia. It houses the remnants of one of the hottest laboratories of the Cold War in Asia, wherein the United States secretly dropped more than 2.7 million tons of bombs, more bombs than the allies dropped in all of World War II. One exhibit, labelled *Bomb House*, gives an account of this planned destruction. The wooden hut's walls are lined with deactivated rockets and an information board displays an archival photo of Richard Nixon pointing at a map of Cambodia. Here stands a technician, the man who turned Cambodia into an experiment in "collateral damage." My mother and father's stories about fleeing the U.S. bombs suddenly come back to me. "To hide from the American bombs, we took shelter under a Buddhist pagoda," my father once told me. After the Khmer Rouge rose to power in the ashes of those bombs, my parents and brothers slept in the fields for almost four years, barely clinging to life. In the hazy afternoon heat, I feel the familiar emotions of anger and bitterness rise in me.

Winding dirt paths cut around the inert weapons, creating a maze for solo travellers and tour groups looking for their fix of the war-ravaged exotic. Cambodian men dressed in blue army uniforms, likely former Khmer Rouge soldiers, offer tours of the surroundings. Many guides carry the wounds of war—prosthetics, bullet wounds, scars—visible for all to see. One guide assembles me and a small group of English-speaking visitors. He tells us: "I spent nearly my whole life in the war. I died more than ten times during the war. They called me a cat. I will show you the scar, the shrapnel, the ball bearing. Everywhere there are holes in my body." At one point during his story, a thirty-something American man in the group, on break from his conference in Chiang Mai, leans over and asks me if I know who Pol Pot is. I have no time for explanations today.

Our guide continues: "They took away my family and then they killed them. I ate the crickets, grasshoppers, frog, fish, snake, everything. A hornet's nest dropped down on me. I live thirty miles north from here. About fifty kilometres. My wife died three years ago. Lung cancer from the uranium.

On April 16, 2017, my friend stepped on a mine and it took off his legs." He takes us to a large ruined tank and peers over the top to point out something inside: "My friend's bones inside. Bowin. He died." I feel a whirling as I listen to him, wishing he would stop, but I am incapable of extracting myself from the group.

I'm jolted out of my daze as our guide ends his monologue to ask our names. I tell him mine, and there is immediate recognition on his part: "You were born in Khao-I-Dang! Khao-I-Dang is the mountain in Thailand. Her name," he says to the group, "is the same as that mountain." The story of my name is a complicated one. KID is the nickname for the refugee camp on the border of Cambodia and Thailand that swelled to the size of a small city back in 1980. Those who made it to this camp were thought to be the most fortunate refugees of the war. Our guide explains: "Some, like your family, when they went to Thailand, were very, very lucky. They got to immigrate, to live in Canada, Australia, New Zealand, the U.S., and Europe, but some were not so lucky. They got repatriated by the United Nations." Then he says to me, "I see that you are a little bit upset, but you will know how lucky you are." I don't know how to respond, to express the sadness I feel in this moment, standing before this man whom I should call bou (*uncle* in Khmer) but don't. Uncle, I want to say, I'm sorry your life has been so hard.

An Australian woman, with two bored and indifferent teenage daughters, jumps in: "Yes, we are very lucky to be Australian, but we have a lot of different cultures that like to bring their cultures into Australia"—laughter from the group—"which is actually the dangerous part."

Our group passes by Chinese-speaking tourists who pose for photos with old rifles and tanks, as if wishing the equipment could be suddenly reanimated. The captions are all in English. More than once a Chinese-speaking passerby stops me, points at something, and asks me in Putonghua, "Zhè shì shénme (這是什麼)"—*What is this?* I shrug and say, "Wǒ bù zhīdào (我不知道)" —*I don't know.*

We come to a crater at the edge of the compound that is fenced off by razor wire but curiously unmarked. Our guide tells us it was caused by the U.S. bombing in 1973, but there is noticeable hesitation in his voice. He doesn't want to linger here, quickly moving us on to the next station. I wonder what in the museum is real and what is fabricated, if it even matters. At the centre of the crater, a little ecosystem has formed, with bright-pink lotus blossoms sprouting up from a pool of lily pads and murky brown water. The Cambodian belief is that the lotus flower emerging from mud symbolizes strength, hope, faith that a new lifeworld can be reborn from the darkest places. I think of the biology of cellular and organic regrowth—that every species, no matter how damaged, is capable of regeneration.

The blazing sun shines in my eyes and time has gotten away from me. Something has both paralyzed me and left me ungrounded. When I arrive at Siem Reap airport, I find I have missed my flight. ▣

In Niger:
A Conversation between
Teju Cole and Joe Penney

PHOTOGRAPHS BY JOE PENNEY

The following pictures are connected to one another by the element of waiting. They are pictures of life, which is inextinguishable, but they are also pictures of hell. What we see here is not a desirable destination: it is a through point, a way station on a terrifying pilgrimage. Here is the misdirection of human possibility, the frustration of what life ought to be, a place of perpetual cross purposes.

Many of the people we see in these pictures are waiting to leave. Many are waiting for things to improve. All are waiting for some kind of explanation for why life should be so hard. The West African nation of Niger, where Joe Penney has for several years paid close and compassionate attention with his camera, is one of the places in the world where the present global predicament (which can be theoretically understood from anywhere) is most directly visible.

Here are the climate migrants, with eyes that long for reunion. Here is American money, the French strategy, and the deadly guesswork of the United Nations. Here is the wreckage that those in distant countries can tolerate, as long as large numbers of other people can be marooned in the antechamber of humanity.

Even when one of those full trucks finally begins to move, the journey is so fearful and the outcome so uncertain that the movement looks like waiting too.

— Teju Cole

Teju Cole: This is an interesting place to start: a quiet shot. You must have had to find a high vantage point.

Joe Penney: Security was on everyone's mind, and people, not knowing who I was, thought I had an ulterior motive. I couldn't get access to any buildings. The sun was setting when I finally met an administrator who let me onto the roof of a government building.

Cole: Do you have specific memories connected to this view?

Penney: The Kennedy Bridge is the main connection between downtown Niamey and Harobanda, the university neighbourhood. Abdoulaye Massalatchi's house in Harobanda had a courtyard with a big neem tree in it, and he would invite my colleague and me over for brochettes and tea. Abdoulaye is a well-travelled journalist. There was only one country, he said, to which he would never return: France.

Penney: This one is in Arlit, in the late afternoon. The setting sun backlit the dust kicked up by motorcycles.

Cole: Why were you in Arlit?

Penney: It is a uranium mining town. Uranium is central to Niger's revenue and essential for France's electricity grid. There are regular power cuts throughout Arlit, but the uranium mined there accounts for a third of the uranium used for nuclear energy in France. We were in Arlit shortly after French workers at the mines were kidnapped by an Al Qaeda–linked group.

Cole: Security must have been a concern.

Penney: Yes. Nigerien national guardsmen accompanied us throughout the trip. I took this picture next to the health clinic run by the French state nuclear energy company Orano, where employees receive basic medical assistance for sometimes mysterious conditions.

Penney: This was in Bilma, an oasis town that is hundreds of years old. The men are a subprefect and his aide, leading us through date trees to an irrigation project to grow vegetables, paid for by European countries.

Cole: How did that project come to be?

Penney: Young men in Bilma drive migrants across the Sahara. The European countries, through the International Organization for Migration (IOM), were looking for incentives to get them to stop.

Cole: There are men on the other side of these trees?

Penney: Yes, working as day labourers paid by IOM. The desert surrounding Bilma is vast, and its immensity puts the self in sharp relief, both emotionally and visually. The date trees of Bilma felt like the opposite of that: tender, cool, and sweet, a natural respite. But I was also thinking about how Europe has so much influence here, to the extent that it is present even in the neighbourhood vegetable garden. The authorities were proud of their work on the irrigation project, but they were also subject to European whims.

Penney: Every week, a military convoy leaves Dirkou, near the Libyan and Chadian borders, and heads southward to Agadez. Civilians being repatriated to their home countries join the convoy for safety. I was travelling with my partner, Ladan, and my colleague, Omar. We left Dirkou around 6 P.M. When we got to a well outside Achegour a couple of hours later, we stopped for the night. The cars you see in the picture are brand new: people buy them in Libya and drive across the desert to sell in Niger and Nigeria. We sat in the pristine sand and made tea. It was August 9.

Cole: The date had some personal significance?

Penney: It was my birthday. I had just turned thirty.

Cole: This is a keen portrait. Who is this man?

Penney: His name is Hassan Mohammed, a former migrant smuggler. He was thirty-one when I took the picture. When Europe tried to stop migration from Africa in 2016, they paid Niger to arrest smugglers. Hassan's whole family used to transport people across the desert, and since the crackdown, two of his cars have been impounded and two of his brothers put in prison. He's lost all his income.

Cole: Who are the other people we see in the picture?

Penney: The other two men are also former smugglers. Most of the smugglers come from families that have been transporting people and goods across the desert for generations. Europe's interference has suppressed trade and in general made it harder for people to cross the Sahara peacefully. Migration was a major industry that benefited many people financially. Hundreds of thousands of West Africans travelled through the country and spent money on food, housing, transportation, bribes. Everyone was getting paid, and it was not a threat to anyone's security. So when Europe came in and shut it down, an entire industry was devastated. Those ople are still struggling to recover. The European set up a program to compensate the smug- tting them out of jobs. In Hassan's case, few bags of expired rice and told y store.

Cole: This image is just so photographically striking to me. Who's this young man, and where was this taken?

Penney: He's a carpenter's apprentice in Agadez. When I photograph stories or breaking news, I also like to shoot scenes of normal life. The thatched roofs in Niger offer really beautiful light patterns and were the impetus for stopping at this carpentry shop during an early-morning walk.

Cole: His mood seems sombre. Is there a story behind that?

Penney: I took a few pictures of the shop's owner before he stepped away and I was able to make a portrait of the apprentice, who was shy and contemplative but willing to be photographed. I appreciate his style, how the pattern of his shirt contrasts the thatched roof shadows on the wall, the paint splotches, and the door against another door.

Penney: This was from a baptism at Omar's family home in Niamey. We often worked together, and I would often hang out with him. His family wanted me to take pictures of their baptism celebration, and of course I was more than happy to do so.

Cole: It is a rare and welcome moment of joy in the set. The composition is pretty dynamic. Were you lying on the ground to get this shot?

Penney: I'm pretty sure I was crouching down to get the shot. I wanted to frame the hand movements of the dancer in the tent, above the women sitting down, so it would stand out more. I'm happy I got a shot when almost everyone was fixated on the dancer and participating as a whole group.

Cole: You really captured it; we are inside their moment without distraction. How do you feel looking at it now?

Penney: Looking at this photo now is emotional for me, especially in a time of isolation and social distancing. The warmth that this image of celebration reminds me of is far away right now, and I hope we can reclaim it soon.

Cole: What was the role of soldiers in the crisis? Are these guys Nigeriens or a multinational force?

Penney: These are Nigerien special forces soldiers, paid by Niger's defence ministry. Each soldier's salary is large enough to raise a family with, but not so much that they can send their kids to school abroad. The soldiers were participating in Flintlock, a yearly American military exercise with African militaries. The American military gathers all the regional armies as well as a bunch of European special forces to emphasize the primacy of American military might.

Cole: What orders were given to the Nigerien soldiers, as far as you could make out? And what was the attitude of the rank-and-file soldiers to the work they were being asked to do?

Penney: American and European special forces train African soldiers in how to set up checkpoints, how to counter ambushes, and other manoeuvres. In 2014, Flintlock was in Diffa, which is a small city in the southeast of the country, on the border with Nigeria. Diffa was at great risk of Boko Haram attack, and these soldiers were meant to be on the front lines fighting Boko Haram after the exercise was over. They were young, underequipped, and scared of being killed. After a certain point, Niger's military handed over the front-line battle against Boko Haram to the Chadian army, and I think everyone was more comfortable with that arrangement.

Cole: Your photos suggest you had pretty good access.

Penney: My colleague and I were embedded with these troops. A day or two after I took these pictures, the American military kicked us off the embed. For the last two days of the five-day trip, we were confined to our rooms. Since we couldn't go out, we invited a local official for an interview at the camp we were staying at. The Nigerien soldiers at the gate checked his credentials and let him in, but when the Americans saw him, they expelled him immediately and berated us for allowing a "potential suicide bomber" into the camp. The Americans didn't speak any French and were very scared of the Nigeriens in general. Many of them wouldn't eat the food the Nigeriens prepared to celebrate the end of the exercise because they thought it might be poisoned.

Cole: Such a striking presence here. This is a nocturnal portrait that, on closer look, seems to depict someone inside a crowd.

Penney: We were at a village about 100 kilometres north of Agadez called Turayat, where migrants passed through in the beginning of their journeys across the desert. Turayat was the last point where you could buy soft drinks, cigarettes, grilled meat, and other goods before heading off into the desert for up to three full days.

Cole: What's that on this man's face?

Penney: Dust. Once you cross the city limits of Agadez, there are no paved roads until Libya. Everyone sits on the back of the truck and faces the elements together. He had taken off a scarf that he was using to cover the rest of his head, which is why the dust forms a pair of goggles over his eyes.

Cole: It's a moving portrait, and the slight blur adds to that feeling. Can you say something about photographing at night in Niger, and how that differed from photographing during the day?

Penney: The light on his face is either from the flashlight of a nearby food vendor or from Omar, who was filming with an LED light on his video camera. In Niger, there's hardly any light pollution and you can clearly see the stars at night, even in Niamey. In a place like Turayat where the night is enveloping, flashlights carry whole beams of light that aren't diffused into other ambient light, creating sharp, relief-like imagery. In contrast, in the daytime I generally stuck to photographing in the early morning and late afternoon, which offered softer, more supple light.

Cole: This one looks like it's from some distant planet. It looks scorching. And what's going on with the scattered wreckage?

Penney: This picture is definitely as hot as it looks. It was taken at the Well of Hope in the Sahara, which is a water point hundreds of miles from the nearest towns. We stopped there when we were coming back to Agadez from Dirkou, and spent more than six hours, from 9 A.M. to 3 P.M., trying to find shade ourselves: under a piece of cloth draped between two cars, inside a crowded building, next to a minivan. The cars have to rest during the hottest parts of the day to make sure the tires don't rip and the engines don't overheat. To keep ourselves hydrated, we mixed electrolyte packets with our water, which had risen in the ambient heat to the temperature of tea. The car debris you see is placed in a circle to delineate the boundaries of a makeshift burial ground for people who have died in the desert. It was an extremely eerie feeling and a reminder of how dangerous travelling in the desert is.

Cole: The name *Well of Hope* sounds like something out of literature. But of course, it's also very real and in this case, as you say, eerie.

Penney: Yes, exactly. Sometimes real life just hits you with the clearest name or metaphor for what you encounter.

Cole: And finally they are on their way.

Penney: Yes. This picture was taken in 2016, when between five and ten thousand people every week were travelling from Niger to Libya on their way to Europe. Later that year, at the behest of Europe, Niger passed a law restricting migrants from moving north and mobilized the Nigerien army to arrest smugglers. The truck is on its way to gold mines near the Libyan border, mines that are now closed down, again at Europe's request because the Europeans thought leaving them open would encourage migration. The truck is taking these migrants from Agadez to the Well of Hope, then on to Dirkou, then Sabha in southern Libya. From Sabha, they will be transferred over to other smugglers, and if they don't get kidnapped or otherwise blocked in Sabha (which is what happens to many of the women), they will head north to Tripoli, Misrata, Zuwara, or one of the other cities along the coast. From there, they will wait in houses or detention centres until they can cross by boat to Italy. Once in Europe, they will move north to where they have families, friends, or other contacts in Germany, France, the U.K., and other European countries.

Cole: This is a very broad question, but what is driving this migration? Why do people want to leave home under such dangerous conditions?

Penney: I can't say for sure what people hope for because everyone has their own individual dreams and desires, but most people I've spoken to making this journey say that first and foremost they want economic stability for themselves and their families. That stability has been denied them in their own countries, often due to the policies put in place by the very European countries they're trying to reach. For a lot of young people making the journey, it's almost a rite of passage. People see their brothers doing it, their cousins, their secondary-school friends on Facebook. Many of those setting out think that they will make it where others have failed. For the most part, people hear success stories; they don't hear about those of their friends who are struggling abroad. That reality is hidden. But enough people who go do raise the quality of their lives and their families' lives by making this trip, and so it remains attractive.

Cole: Your photographs are witness to a kind of limbo and to a kind of monumental waste: a waste of people's efforts, of their time, of their possibilities.

Penney: I often think this odyssey is entirely unnecessary, and that it is much more dangerous and expensive than simply getting on a flight. Western countries cannot ignore the humanity of others forever, given how interwoven we all are. Much of southern Europe's agricultural sector, for instance, relies on undocumented West African labour, but there's been little honesty about this. I think Europe's fate hinges on its ability to deal with its whiteness. Western countries will need to move past their racism if they want to survive, though it's hard to believe that this vision of the future can be a reality. But it must become a reality. Leoluca Orlando, the mayor of Palermo, told me, "The migrants are giving us a new idea of freedom," in that they are challenging countries to build societal identities on shared values instead of shared bloodlines. To meet that challenge, Niger needs to be free, but so does Europe, in a new and more just way. B̅

A Note on Jane Jacobs's *Systems of Survival*, or Why We Will Not Be Able to Prevent Global Ecological Collapse

JAN ZWICKY

At key points in the *Republic*, Plato's great dialogue about how to remedy injustice in the individual soul and in the state at large, we find reference to seeking "to outdo others." To want to outdo others is to be governed by *pleonexia*, a desire for more and more, a desire for more than enough. Pleonexia, Plato argues, is the root of injustice; it leads to wanting what isn't yours. To be just, by contrast, is to want to have and to do only, and exactly, what is your own. Justice can be achieved, Plato suggests, through the coordinated exercise of three other virtues: self-restraint, courage, and wisdom. He intended the *Republic* not just as a portrait of the ideal state and fully moral individual, but also as a critique of existing attitudes and methods of government. It failed to save the day. By the time Plato wrote it, the brutal and bloated Athenian empire was sliding irretrievably into chaos. The American empire—another brutal and pleonectic culture—is also collapsing, and the disintegration of a "progressive" world order is taking place amid the biospheric catastrophe that it has spawned. It is too late, as it was too late in Plato's Athens, to urge the virtues of self-restraint and wisdom on the state. We are left to attempt meaningful moral gestures as individuals and small communities rather than as voting members of large national polities.

The virtue now most required by those of us who enjoy the supermarkets, the drinkable tap water, and the air conditioning offered by Western so-called liberal democracies is courage: courage to admit our individual complicity in ecological catastrophe and courage to admit that we belong to a remarkably violent, intemperate, and short-sighted species. These acts of self-recognition may, in turn, give us the integrity to die well.

Are there special "ecological" virtues that we ought to have practised? No. If we look at surviving stories from Paleolithic cultures, we see that there is significant overlap between the virtues they praise and the virtues praised by Neolithic cultures. Indeed, there is significant overlap among the virtues admired in Paleolithic cultures and those advocated by monotheistic religions. The core set is the same as Plato's: courage, self-restraint, sagacity or wisdom, and justice. That these four canonical virtues have been repeatedly urged on us for millennia suggests that humans as a species are prone to greed, to cheating, to rash and stupid behaviour, and to refusing to face up to these facts about ourselves. Stories promoting the canonical virtues, bolstered by warnings about the consequences of failing to observe them, are meant to make communal life possible, and to help humans live equitably, not only with each other but with the rest of the world's inhabitants—on whose well-being their own well-being depends.

However, all cultures also attest to a list of shadow virtues: trickery and thievery; impulsive bravado; clever deceit; ham-fisted violence in males, as long as it's powerful enough to suppress opposition; and vanity in females, as long as it secures them a mate. We see pleonexia operating in one form or another in all of them. I call them *virtues* because they are traits that are admired and cultivated, indeed regarded as forms of human excellence. I call them *shadow* virtues because, although this admiration is real, it is covert. The shadow virtues are rarely explicitly acknowledged as admirable: thievery isn't thievery if everyone agrees to it; deceit isn't deceit unless its practitioner pretends honesty; vanity that parades itself openly is usually regarded as pitiable or disgusting. Where admiration is explicit, these shadow virtues are consolidated in trickster figures and in stories of male aggression in war.

It is the triumph of the shadow virtues, sustained and promoted by advertising (itself often a form of clever deceit), that has led to global environmental

© Jacques Oulé

catastrophe. The old stories have always warned us of the consequences of succumbing to shadow ideals, and they have always told us that it's in our nature to think we can get away with flouting the canonical virtues until it's too late.

Whence these shadow virtues? Why are they so resistant to control by the canonical virtues? How is it that, intelligent though we are, they are proving our—and many other species'—undoing?

In *Systems of Survival*, Jane Jacobs describes two distinct constellations of human virtues that show up pan-culturally, at least in urbanized cultures. So-called "traders" condemn violence and value cooperation, transparency, and social equality; so-called "guardians"

condemn trading and value the hierarchical organization of power, displays of prowess, secrecy, and an us-versus-them approach to the world. Examples of guardian institutions in global corporate consumer culture include the Mafia, the NSA, CSIS, the military, some religious orders, industrial monopolies, the police, aristocracies, government bureaucracies; and they used to include symphony orchestras and the academy. Traders "institutionalize" less often; the style is epitomized in the person running a small, innovative business, or volunteer collectives seeking to better their communities.

Here are Jacobs's lists of the characteristics associated with each moral paradigm:

The Trader Moral Syndrome	*The Guardian Moral Syndrome*
shun force	shun trading
come to voluntary agreements	exert prowess
be honest	be obedient and disciplined
collaborate easily with strangers	be exclusive
compete	respect hierarchy
respect contracts	take vengeance
use initiative and enterprise	be loyal
be open to inventiveness and novelty	adhere to tradition
be efficient	make rich use of leisure
promote comfort and convenience	show fortitude
dissent for the sake of the task	deceive for the sake of the task
invest for productive purposes	treasure honour
be industrious	dispense largesse
be thrifty	be ostentatious
be optimistic	be fatalistic

Jacobs discovered the two moral constellations as she puzzled over intractable problems facing North American society: the expansion of bureaucracies that waste everyone's time; the growth of ethnic tensions; our inability to trust a word our politicians utter; the persistence of vast nuclear arsenals. She decided to research the morality governing "practical working life" to see if she could figure out why these problems resisted solution. Her reading was extensive and wide-ranging. It included biographies, business histories, reports of scandals, sociology, history, and cultural anthropology. Both syndromes, Jacobs claims, share a number of "universal" virtues, which she lists separately: courage, moderation, wisdom, common sense, competence, cooperation, foresight, judgment, perseverance, faith, energy, patience, and mercy.

Three of the four canonical virtues—moderation (self-restraint), courage, and wisdom—appear explicitly in this list. But they appear there under other names as well. That is, I think the list can be condensed. Perseverance, patience, and energy are specific forms of courage, inflected in the cases of perseverance and patience by self-restraint; faith, too, is a form of self-restraint—the refusal to succumb to despair; common sense, foresight, judgment, and competence are all forms of sagacity or wisdom. This leaves cooperation and mercy unaccounted for—as allegedly universal virtues over and above the canonical four. But I am not convinced that either is, in fact, universally regarded as a virtue. Cooperation is the *paradigmatic* trader virtue and is frequently dismissed as irrelevant by those who subscribe to a guardian ethos. Think of the stories that involve rogue cops or cowboys fighting for justice on their own terms,

no part of a community, never working with others. And mercy appears to be a virtue associated with monotheistic religions: a curb on patriarchal rage. This is what distinguishes it from compassion, its trader complement—mercy is exercised in contexts in which there is a judicially determined right to behave cruelly. Trader communities rarely recognize such a right. In guardian cultures, mercy is frequently dispensed opportunistically, to cement loyalty in the one to whom mercy is shown. I propose, then, that we add cooperation to the list of specifically trader virtues and mercy to the list of specifically guardian virtues.

The other outstanding discrepancy between Jacobs's list of universal virtues and the standard four is the absence of justice from Jacobs's list. Consider, though, those lists of non-universal virtues, the ones that distinguish Jacobs's two paradigms. It seems to me that in several cases, what we see are the "universal" virtues—including justice—refracted through two distinct lenses: justice *as* respect for contracts and justice *as* vengeance; self-control *as* thrift or efficiency and self-control *as* obedience; wisdom *as* honesty and openness to innovation, and wisdom *as* adherence to tradition; courage *as* willingness to collaborate and to dissent, and courage *as* prowess and fatalistic fortitude. What determines the guise in which a "universal" virtue becomes manifest? It appears that what we might at first be tempted to call "moral frameworks" are, in fact, ecologies of sorts—organizations in which the parts inflect one another. Within a given moral ecology, so-called universal virtues may appear as themselves, but they may also take on inflections determined by their interactions within the whole. In their inflected versions, if Jacobs is correct, they are complemented and reinforced by other distinct virtues.

One striking feature of the lists is the degree of conflict they suggest. It is indeed little wonder that situations in which both paradigms are operating are beset by insoluble problems. Another striking feature is the presence of several shadow virtues—trickery, deceit, violence—on the guardian list.

It is, however, even more striking that pleonexia shows up—under more than one name—on both lists. In guardian mode, we *admire* ostentation and displays of largesse; we *admire* those who lie their way into power or profit and who hang on to it with an iron fist. On the other hand, if we're in a trader frame of mind, we're happy to promote excess in the guise of comfort and convenience—the marketing and consumption of useless gadgetry and of novelty for novelty's sake. "Shopping," as it used to say on the doors of the Bay in Victoria, B.C., "is good." How is conspicuous consumption to be reconciled with the trader virtue of thrift? Perhaps it isn't. Perhaps we are witnessing the erosion of the trader moral code under the relentless metastasis of capitalism. But note that marketers still appeal to thrift in an effort to encourage overconsumption: everything everywhere is declared to be On Sale! at Rock Bottom Prices! And we succumb, occasionally experiencing subsequent bewilderment at the useless stuff crowding our cupboards. Then there's capitalism itself: the unrestrained exploitation of natural "resources" that undergirds the shibboleth of economic growth: pleonexia in the form of so-called productive investment.

When I look at the lists further, I notice something else. Although I'm willing to believe that the syndromes are exhibited panculturally in contemporary urbanized societies, it seems they may not have been present (and may not be present now) in all societies everywhere. They may, for instance, have been absent in at least some native North American societies at the time of European contact. I'm thinking, for example, of the Haudenosaunee and Algonquian societies described in the seventeenth-century *Relations des Jésuites de la Nouvelle-France*. In those societies, collaboration with strangers, cooperation, and optimism appear to have coexisted comfortably with exertion of prowess, the treasuring of honour, respect for tradition, and loyalty. Does such a merging of the two lists represent a third sort of moral culture? Or a collapse of distinct syndromes under certain economic and territorial conditions? Does it show that where pleonexia is made impossible by scarcity of resources, the two moral codes do not diverge? I do not know. But I think it would be worth trying to find out.

Why do we collectively fail to enact the canonical virtues in their canonical forms, even when our lives or the lives of our children depend on it? What Jacobs's syndromes suggest is that the answer arises from conflict between and within our practical moral codes.

In the first instance, change on the scale required would mean a sudden wholesale shift to a predominantly trader ethos: honesty from those in corporate and political power; massive cooperation both locally and internationally; collaboration with strangers; thrift of a profound character—which would mean openness to radical changes in lifestyle for those in rich countries. The guardians among us experience demands for this kind of behaviour as intuitively *wrong*. We can't expect them cheerfully to substitute thrift for ostentatious display; we can't expect those who occupy positions of corporate and political power—and there are many, for power, maintained by backroom deals and loyal cabals, is the guardian's native turf—suddenly to own up to the actual state of the resource base.

The second source of disabling conflict lies within the trader ethos itself. Pleonexia shows up not just in the form of ostentatious guardian largesse but also in the form of trader-driven consumerism. Really to encourage the necessary thrift would require restraint on investment, an overturning of the ideal of endless economic "growth," and an overhaul of wealthy notions of comfort, convenience, and the pursuit of novelty. In addition, those of us who've been living beyond our ecological means would need to cultivate guardian-style fortitude in the face of an end to luxury.

We'd also need a good dose of fatalism to balance the compulsory optimism that imagines there's a high-tech solution just around the corner. But part of what is entailed by the fact that the syndromes are *ecologies* is that we can't just cookie-cut the specific virtues we need. To modify any given aspect is to modify all.

How deep do the tensions go? If it weren't for the Paleolithic record, I would suspect they were biological. And we must remember that even Paleolithic cultures were rich in stories whose moral is the need for self-restraint. The pleonectic shadow virtues appear to be idealizations of desire. And why not? Desire goes very deep in the history of life on this planet; it is arguably part of the definition of life. If this is so, then humans turn out to be a moderately disastrous and ultimately self-cancelling evolutionary experiment—a form of life, a version of wanting, that got too good at getting. ◨

An Interview with Masha Gessen

ELEANOR WACHTEL

Masha Gessen was born into a Jewish family in Moscow in 1967. At the age of fourteen, they emigrated with their family to the United States, where within just a few years they began working as a journalist, reporting for a gay newspaper in Boston.

A decade after arriving in the U.S., Gessen returned to Russia on assignment to cover the dynamic, tumultuous times—what turned out to be a brief period of democracy—after the collapse of the Soviet Union. That stay in Moscow lasted twenty-two years, until Putin's anti-gay crackdown forced Gessen to emigrate again, back to New York, which remains home.

A staff writer and columnist for the New Yorker, *Masha Gessen is also a prolific contributor to the* New York Times, *the* New York Review of Books, *the* Washington Post, Vanity Fair, *and many other publications, as well as the author of ten non-fiction books, including* Ester and Ruzya: How My Grandmothers Survived Hitler's War and Stalin's Peace, The Man Without a Face: The Unlikely Rise of Vladimir Putin, Words Will Break Cement: The Passion of Pussy Riot, *and most recently,* The Future Is History: How Totalitarianism Reclaimed Russia, *which won the 2017 National Book Award for Nonfiction. The* Washington Post *described* The Future Is History *as "a sweeping intellectual history of Russia over the past four decades, told through a Tolstoyan gallery of characters." This June, Gessen will be coming out with a further analysis of Trumpism, called* Surviving Autocracy.

Hailed for astute and incisive analysis of both Russian and American abuses of power, Gessen once said that their family's traumatic experiences in the upheavals of the twentieth century gave them the "catastrophic imagination" so many Americans lack. The recipient of numerous awards, including a Guggenheim Fellowship and an Andrew Carnegie Fellowship, Gessen is the John J. McCloy Professor of American Institutions and International Diplomacy at Amherst College.

Last November, I was invited by the Socrates Project at McMaster University to interview Masha Gessen on stage as part of its Living Democracy series.

Eleanor Wachtel: Your father was a computer scientist, your mother a writer and translator. When you were fourteen, you emigrated from the Soviet Union with your family to the United States, but before that, as you say, your parents were dissident sympathizers. How would that play out in your home?

Masha Gessen: Dissidents were politically persecuted for thinking differently. So usually you were considered a dissident when you actually suffered severe repercussions, such as being jailed or being forcibly exiled from the country, which is not what happened to us; we left voluntarily. A lesser version would be being fired from your job and left without a means of existence, often being internally exiled and not being allowed to live in the city. For a small group of people, a small and measurable group of people, the repercussions for dissident activism were huge. It was a life-defining activity.

But there was a wider circle of people who followed everything the dissidents did, read everything the dissidents published underground, and circulated books and periodicals that were published abroad, but who took enough care to try not to get caught and never directly confronted the regime. And I'd say that my parents belonged to that wider circle of people. It was not risk-free by any stretch of the imagination, but it was not a terrifying kind of existence, and there was no certainty that you would go to jail, as there was with actual dissidents.

The way it played out in our home . . . the most memorable event was when I was four years old, after we had just moved into this new apartment in a huge apartment block. The neighbour rang the bell, and I opened the door and said, "I'm sorry, my parents can't come to the door. They're busy typing Solzhenitsyn." I can only surmise that my parents kept waving me away because they were taking turns at the typewriter. Typewriters were pretty scarce, and usually anything you could copy by typing was also fairly scarce, so they were probably trying to speed-type a copy of some piece by Solzhenitsyn, or maybe even a book, I don't know, and they were taking turns at the typewriter as they got tired, to try to do it as fast as possible before they had to take the original to whoever was supposed to have it next. So I was probably getting kicked out of their room as they were typing, and so I was like, "They're busy, they're typing Solzhenitsyn, we can't bother them right now." And then all hell broke loose: my parents started running around, slamming doors, saying that they didn't know what I said, and that's probably my first memory of the power of the written word.

Wachtel: In 1991 you went back to Russia as an American journalist and ended up staying in Moscow. You said you were surprised at how comfortable and relaxed you felt after being away for a decade. I wonder what you were expecting.

Gessen: I was expecting to be in a foreign country where I happened to speak the language. At that point, it had only been ten years, but it was a big deal: the ten years that passed were from the ages of fourteen to twenty-four. I was very much an American journalist. I'd done a couple of foreign assignments, and so I thought, Okay, I'm going to have a leg up because I speak the language and other people don't, but I wasn't following Soviet politics very closely, and I didn't have strong social connections with some family back in Moscow, so I expected to kind of parachute in on assignment and come out. And I was blindsided by feeling at home.

Wachtel: I was surprised to read that, given that you had assimilated as an American. You spent many formative years in the U.S., and you were going back as a journalist to cover what was, as you've said, the most exciting place in the world, as the Soviet regime was collapsing. What was it about Russia that made you feel at home?

Gessen: I don't know, but I think there are physical features of childhood that you never quite leave behind. I think it has to do with the way the light falls and the way the air smells, and just physically inhabiting a space. I mean, I love living in New York. I lived in New York as a young person, and I live back in New York now. When I step onto the sidewalk in New York, it just fills me with energy. But it's a different feeling. It's a variety of an at-home feeling, but it's different from a mould that was there waiting for me to fit back into it.

Wachtel: A Masha-sized space was waiting.

Gessen: Exactly. A Masha-sized space was waiting, and that's a very bizarre feeling because it's not like I was particularly welcome, and it's not like it was the easiest place for me to be socially—somebody who's a little suspect for having lived in the States, and someone who's a lot suspect for being queer and for being Jewish—so maybe it's a kind of masochism. There's a great line in my brother's book. My brother is the writer Keith Gessen, and he wrote a novel called *A Terrible Country* that's loosely based on his experience of going back to Moscow in 2008 to stay with our grandmother while I was on a fellowship in the States. I'd asked him to come to Moscow and hang out for the year, so he went. There's a fictional character in the book, the narrator's older brother, who's very unlikeable, but I try not to take it personally. Anyways, it's a lovely novel. I like it in part because you can tell that the narrator really loves this unlikeable guy, adores his older brother who's a total asshole. At one point the narrator describes his older brother—who's tiny, Jewish, and unlike anybody there—and he says this great line: "He knew no one liked him, and it put him at ease." And I thought, this might be a bit biographical.

Wachtel: Along with the Masha-sized space, there were your grandmothers waiting for you at the airport when you went back to Moscow. Ester was your father's mother and Ruzya your maternal grandmother. Can you talk about the role they played in your growing up?

Gessen: Grandmothers are very important in Russian culture and Jewish culture and Soviet culture because everybody works and child care is spotty, so grandmothers are expected to be very much a part of the child-rearing. But I had very different relationships with my maternal and paternal grand-mothers, and here's the strange thing: they were best friends, and they had been best friends for many years before my parents got married. My parents met as children because their mothers were best friends. So I was very confused about the whole family thing. The idea that families came together from different places and that other people's families had two sides didn't occur to me until I was an adult, probably. I just thought family was like a glob that moves together because all my aunts were friends and they all went to school together. So my grandmothers existed in this very close relationship and in a kind of best-friend opposition to each other, and it was this opposition that I started discovering when I went back and started talking to them. This was the weird sort of luxury of getting to re-meet them after ten years. Things that would have been completely familiar to me, that wouldn't have occurred to me to ask them about, had become estranged enough that I could recognize them for the stories they were. I started interviewing my grandmothers almost as soon as I went back to the Soviet Union, and then about ten years later I wrote a book called *Ester and Ruzya—*

Wachtel: *How My Grandmothers Survived Hitler's War and Stalin's Peace.* When you say interviewed, like, really interviewed?

Gessen: I really interviewed them, yeah. I would show up with a Dictaphone, and I would interview them, and the experience was very different in both cases. One of my grandmothers, Ester, is this amazing storyteller, and all her stories were perfectly encapsulated, and no matter what I did she would always tell the stories in exactly the same way with the same punchline. I would point out contradictions to her and she would just not see them because the story had taken shape years before and this was the only way it was going to exist. And interviewing my grandmother Ruzya was, in a way, much more interesting because she's one of those very unusual people who goes back and relives the thing that you're asking them about, and I've only had that experience a few times in my life, when somebody really re-experiences the thing. So when I interviewed her about the same events on different occasions—because I did these interviews over a number of years, I did this quite purposefully; I would interview them about the same thing several times—she would tell really different stories, and that was amazing. In a way, it was much harder to write, but it was an amazing interviewing experience.

There was a family mythology that Ruzya, my maternal grandmother, was kind of a collaborator. Not in a terrible way, but in a normal Soviet way. She was not a dissident, and she did what was necessary to survive, and what was necessary to survive was being a part of the totalitarian machine. She worked as a censor for foreign correspondents accredited in Moscow from 1946 until 1957. So then I came back as a foreign correspondent and interviewed her about being a censor for foreign correspondents.

Wachtel: But in her defence—because I find her such an interestingly complex person—she was trained as a history teacher, and she didn't feel she could do that.

Gessen: Well, that's just the thing. And my other grandmother was considered the rebel who had never compromised. As I got into these stories, they turned out to be so much more complicated because the grandmother who was the censor, by the time she got her degree in history, she decided she could not work as a history teacher because she couldn't lie to children, and so her moral choice was to take a job as a censor, and the way she explained it was that censorship was kind of a mechanical job. Anybody in Ruzya's position would have done the same thing. She worked behind the curtain using just her pencil. I mean, literally. Foreign correspondents would come into this place and hand over their dispatch, and then someone would take it behind the curtain where my grandmother sat, and she would cross stuff out and it would be brought back out to the correspondent, who could then file it. If she'd been a history teacher, she would have used her whole being to lie to children, and all her ability to be beautiful and charming and funny would have been a part of the machine, and she didn't want to do that, so she chose to be a censor. And it got even more complicated because she hated the job but loved the job because it was so interesting, and she learned languages, and she had access to information that other people couldn't access.

As I interviewed my other grandmother, Ester, the one who once refused to collaborate under threat of death, I learned that she had once accepted a job with the MGB, the precursor to the KGB, as a translator, but then she didn't pass the medical exam because she turned out to be blind in one eye. So she narrowly escaped being a collaborator, actually working for the Security Ministry, and she got to maintain the self-concept of somebody who never collaborated.

Wachtel: Both your grandmothers and your mother worked as translators, and they also edited and wrote. Was it a given that you would end up in the family business?

Gessen: Not at all. Translation is incredibly hard work, and they loved translating. My maternal grandmother could talk for hours about how she was addicted to translating, and my mom also really loved translating, but at the same time I think they felt like it was the fallback profession. At one point my mother warned me that if I kept doing a bit of everything and didn't focus on one thing, I was going to end up a translator like her. Little did she know that that's actually what journalists do.

Wachtel: You worked on the acclaimed television series *The Americans*, translating the dialogue for the Russian characters from the English script. It was a story about a Soviet couple, spies who are planted in the United States in the 1980s, and they have children and an apparently American life. You said, "My life prepared me to do one job, and this was it." Why was it such a great fit for you?

Gessen: Well, this is pretty funny. This is my ultimate claim to fame, that I was the translator on *The Americans*. I was still living in Moscow when *The Americans* first came out, and I thought it was absolutely brilliant. I'd never seen such insight into the psychology of growing up in a totalitarian society, but also serving the Soviet state, and then the interaction of Soviet people and Americans, and it's also just a very beautifully written television show that is mostly about things that are not spoken, which is so unusual. In American television, everything is articulated over and over again, and this was just slow and subtle and gorgeous and blew me away.

After the first couple of seasons, there was a very large contingent of Russian speakers who were watching it in English. And the Russian scenes are in

Russian, so we were all complaining to one another, often on social media, about how terrible the Russian in the series was. So then I got an email from Anne Applebaum, the Pulitzer Prize–winning author of *Gulag*, who clearly was also part of this club of the disaffected watchers of *The Americans*, saying, "*The Americans* are looking for a new translator. Do you have any recommendations?" And by this point I was living in New York, and I started looking around and asking people if they might know somebody. And I thought, That's what I really want to do. I went to talk to the showrunners, and they thought I was a bit crazy, but they said, "Okay, if you really want to do this, let's do it," and I did it for the last three seasons of the show. And the reason I said that my life prepared me for it was that the stories of these people . . . they were sent to the United States to be sleeper agents in the late 1960s as young people, and they become active in the 1980s. There are a bunch of Russian characters around them who are all 1980s Soviet citizens who speak Russian. Russian changed drastically when the Soviet Union collapsed. It absorbed a lot of English words, it developed a lot of new slang, and people who lived continuously in the Russian-speaking world often can't remember when a word appeared in the language. I remember it very well because I went back to Russia in 1991, and I have a strong recollection of all the words I had to learn that I couldn't understand or that I was using the Russian words for, but Russian had already absorbed the English. So I'm one of the few people who have a living Russian language on the one hand and on the other hand have this gap in the 1980s. You can't google "Did this word exist in the 1980s?" And you had to translate the dialogue written in English into believable 1980s Soviet speech. I mean, when I say "you had to," it's just because the showrunners were such purists.

Wachtel: They were amazingly assiduous because most of the American audience wouldn't know the difference. They all read the subtitles, which were in English, from the Russian that you wrote from the English script.

Gessen: It was almost completely art for art's sake, but I think there's something to that kind of obsession with authenticity that probably helps explain why the show was so profoundly good, so deeply, genuinely good.

Wachtel: Throughout this series, the spies, Elizabeth and Philip, had different responses to their life in the U.S. Elizabeth still had strong ties to the Soviet Union, while Philip embraced the American way of life, and this seemed to parallel your own parents.

Gessen: I don't know if it paralleled my own parents. I mean, I think both of my parents liked living in the States. There's a kind of tragic plot to the lives of all of these Soviet émigrés who left in the 1980s, which is that everybody decided to take this drastic step of leaving, usually leaving their parents behind, sometimes leaving other loved ones behind, thinking they will never be able to see them because they believed the Soviet regime was going to exist forever. And then ten years after we came to the U.S., it collapsed, and I think for my mom, who was a literary critic and translator, it was a source of deep regret. They could have waited out the five years until perestroika began, and then she would have had the most interesting work in the universe if she had stayed. I think for my dad it was very different. He really found himself in the kind of clichéd entrepreneurial spirit of the United States. He loves it here, he loved it here, he fit in. So it's not that my mom was nostalgic like Elizabeth for the Soviet state. She was nostalgic for her friends and her intellectual and literary milieu, and my dad really liked the cars, kind of like Philip.

Wachtel: You published an unauthorized biography of Putin in 2012 called *The Man Without a Face: The Unlikely Rise of Vladimir Putin*. The biography came out and it was a big success: it came out in twenty languages; it was a bestseller. Six months later, you met him. What happened?

Gessen: I should say it's not very often you write a book about somebody and then they call you. And it wasn't the first time I wrote a book about somebody whom I didn't have a chance to talk to. Before that, I had written a book about the mathematician Grigori Perelman, who proved the Poincaré conjecture and then disappeared and wouldn't talk to anybody.

Wachtel: He also declined a million-dollar prize.

Gessen: He declined a million-dollar prize and continued to live in poverty and obscurity, and he quit mathematics. So I probably would have been more excited if he had called me, but Putin was pretty exciting as well. I had this sort of double life as a Russian journalist after I went back as a correspondent. In a couple of years, I started writing in Russian as well and had a career as a political reporter in Russian; and then, when political journalism became untenable, I followed my other passion, which is science writing. I was editor of a popular science journal, the oldest continuously published magazine in Russia, the highest-circulation magazine in Russia, a very big-deal kind of magazine. The reason I mention this is because it was a big enough deal that Putin read it and liked it, and when he likes something, he thinks he owns it. And at one point, he wished for a reporter to accompany him while he went hang-gliding with the Siberian cranes.

Wachtel: Siberian cranes?

Gessen: Siberian cranes, yes. On a Saturday morning, my publisher called me and said, "You need to send a reporter," and I said, "Can we not do that?" This was not a brave journalistic stand; it was actually the opposite. I said, "Look, if we send a reporter, the reporter's going to see something that you don't want in the magazine, but I'm going to have to publish it. We're a popular science magazine: we don't have to do this." And he said, "No, they really want a reporter. How about you send a reporter and then we don't publish anything?" I said, "That I can't do." He said, "Okay, you're fired." So I got fired on Saturday morning. On Monday, I went in to work, I signed all the papers concerning the conditions of my obsolescence, and I tweeted that I was leaving. I tweeted, "I'm leaving the magazine. You can thank Putin for that," which is part of a long-running meme about things that we thank Putin for, like, you know, the sun coming out. And so there was still a bit of a free media in Russia, and I got a bunch of phone calls and people wrote about it, and the next morning, Putin called me and said, "I hear you got fired and I was unwittingly at fault." And I thought, Okay, this is a prank, and I have to come up with something really witty to say because when they post this on YouTube, I have to sound good. Then he said, "I just want you to know that I'm sincere about my nature-conservation efforts, and ideally this should be kept separate from politics, but for a person in my position, that's very difficult." And I thought, This guy is so good. I had spent years listening to everything he ever said, and it's one thing to be able to imitate a voice, but it's another thing to imitate a whole way of thinking and making yourself sympathetic. I thought, This person is brilliant; this person must have spent more time in Putin's head than I have. And then he said, "Can we meet?" And I said, "Sure, but how do I know that you are who you say you are?" And then he actually cracked up, and he said, "Well, after we hang up you're going to get a phone call from the deputy head of my administration, and he's going to schedule a meeting, and you're going to come to the Kremlin, and I'm going to be there, and then you'll know." And I said, "Okay," and I thought, This is all going to sound horrible on YouTube. But it turned out to actually be Putin, and he wanted to offer me my job back, which wasn't his to offer back, but he didn't realize this. And in a way, it *was* his to offer back because of course if he said that I was editor again, I would be editor again. But the experience for me was really interesting because it was like having a character that I'd written come to life, and I really wanted to see whether it was the same character. Part of me wanted to be right because the character in my book wasn't very interesting—he was kind of uncurious, uneducated, dull, and dumb—but another part of me wanted him to be more interesting. I wanted to be charmed, I wanted to make a connection with this person whom I spent so much time thinking about, but he turned out to be exactly the person I described in the book.

Wachtel: And he didn't know about the book, or did he know by the time he met you?

Gessen: This was fascinating. He didn't know about the book, and he actually wasn't briefed at all. There were many things that he didn't know. He didn't know that I was a U.S. citizen, he didn't know that I'd had a long-standing record as an opposition journalist, and he didn't know about the book. And there's an explanation for this, which is that someone would have had to tell him. I mean, he doesn't use the internet, and he doesn't use a computer at all. He gets all his information in printouts in large letters, like fourteen-point.

Wachtel: Seriously?

Gessen: Yeah, seriously. I'm a journalist.

Wachtel: I believe you, I believe you.

Gessen: He didn't know any of this stuff before because why would anybody tell him there was this book published about him in twenty languages that was highly critical? That would be a very unpleasant experience telling him about this, and he's not going to find out otherwise. Then after he called me, nobody wanted to tell him because it would be an even less pleasant experience to tell him that he'd scheduled a meeting with this person who had written this book and who was an opposition journalist and who's an American citizen. So there was this jockeying between the administration and the press office, and the press office, I think, wanted to avoid getting in trouble for not having told him this stuff, so they needed to take over the meeting.

That experience actually makes it easier for me to digest the impeachment hearings now because that kind of competition between agencies within an administration . . . in Russia it was grotesque. Nobody is trying to pursue the national interest. Everybody's pursuing their own interest and trying to protect their own jobs. In the States, we have a different situation where there's one set of people, each of whom basically has their own gamble—but are also mostly protecting themselves, their jobs, and their boss's job—and another group who are trying to work according to some logical way of doing their work, and it's like two non-intersecting realities.

Wachtel: I want to come back to that shortly, but to stay with Putin for a moment, you said he set out to create a mafia state, not a totalitarian state, but somehow the two merged. Why?

Gessen: That's what *The Future Is History* is about. It's kind of a long argument, but *mafia state* is a term that was pioneered by my favourite contemporary political thinker, a Hungarian sociologist named Bálint Magyar, who has an extraordinary life story. He was a dissident sociologist in the 1980s, he was a member of the liberal Hungarian government in the 1990s, he became part of the opposition when the Orban governments came to power in the aughts, and then he went back to sociology. And he's basically spent more than a decade trying to figure out how to think about these autocracies, mostly in Eastern Europe, although I think at this point a lot of his work is not directly applicable to what's going on in Western democracies, but some of it is transferable and certainly the language that he has introduced is incredibly useful. The irony of it is that his original insight was that the language we use to describe Eastern European countries, which is the language of liberal democracy, is hugely misleading. The way

he puts it is: in 1989, we all just decided that these countries were going to become liberal democracies because we'd won the Cold War. That was just the assumption: "end of history," the whole thing. And then to some extent, some countries did become liberal democracies, and most of them didn't, and others reverted, and we started talking about them still in the language of liberal democracy, saying that they don't have a free press, or they don't have fair and open elections. And Magyar says that's like saying that the elephant can't swim, or the elephant can't fly. It doesn't tell you anything about the elephant, it just tells you about a few things that it isn't, which may not even be key to its essence.

So he described the Hungarian regime—and it also describes the Russian regime, and he believes this as well—as a mafia state. And it's distinct from any state that we've seen before in that it is run by a clan with a patron at the centre who distributes money and power. It's not crony capitalism because there's no transaction there. It's not like you give me a little bit and I give you a little bit, and it's a system of favours. No: it's distributive. He controls it all, and he allows you to have some power and some money as long as he wants you to have it. It's also a clan, which is like a mafia family. You can be born into the family, or you can be adopted into the family, but you can't bribe your way into the family. You can't join the family by applying to the family, and you also can't leave the family voluntarily. We've learned a lot about what happens to people who try to leave the family when the family doesn't want to be left. They end up being found dead in a Washington hotel, for example. So the mafia state is post-ideological. It uses ideology instrumentally.

Occasionally we see Putin give an ideological speech. After the annexation of Crimea, he gave this speech that sounded very much like Hitler's speech after the annexation of Sudetenland, but most of the time he's just talking about pragmatics and boring stuff. He's not ideologically driven. He's driven entirely by the desire to maintain and enlarge money and power. And this I think is an important concept as well: the interest they're following is not some perverted idea of a national interest. It is entirely self-interested, and this distinguishes it from totalitarian regimes, which have a bizarre idea of the national interest, but it's an idea of the national interest. And it's obvious why some of this is extremely useful for thinking about Trump because I don't think Trump thinks there's a national interest that he's perverting. Trump is entirely driven by the possibility of using the president's office in his own interests, and he basically believes that power exists for the purpose of distributing money and power, and for no other purpose.

What happened in Russia is that Putin set out to build a mafia state, and for a while it was really quite easy to create this mafia state, basically up until about 2012. For the first thirteen years in power, he had a very easy time of it because there was a trade-off. Eight years of that time, between 2000 and 2008, were years of unprecedented prosperity in Russia. Even with the accumulation of money at the top, enough of it was trickling down that everybody was living better, so there was a trade-off: you leave the regime alone, the regime leaves you alone, and you get to live much better, which is the authoritarian model. Basically, authoritarians, unlike totalitarians, want people to stay at home, tend to their private lives, and not pay attention to how the country is run. Totalitarians want the opposite: they want the people out in the public square demonstrating their support.

And then in 2011 to 2012, protests broke out. That bargain was not working anymore, and Putin started cracking down in the interest of the mafia state, but the society that he was cracking down on has such a strong memory of totalitarianism. Everybody in it was so shaped by Soviet totalitarianism that the society responded by reconstituting itself as a totalitarian society, which is very easy to manipulate. It's great ground for a mafia state because people will horizontally enforce everything and will police one another, and the state doesn't even have to do it. That's why the subtitle of the book is *How Totalitarianism Reclaimed Russia*. I don't think Russia has a totalitarian regime, but I think the lived experience of being in Russia now is the lived experience of living in a totalitarian society.

Wachtel: In Putin's moves to consolidate power, he needed a common enemy for Russians to hate and fear, and he chose the LGBTQ community, although there were, as you've pointed out, other groups that were discriminated against or persecuted, such as Muslims or Chechens. Why did the gay community in Russia become such a target?

Gessen: I think that an honest answer is twofold. One is that it's random, and the choice of the scapegoat of minority is always random, so I don't want to say that we're the chosen people because—

Wachtel: Been there, done that.

Gessen: Exactly. On the other hand, and this is true not just of Putin: a lot of autocrats and aspiring autocrats are finding that LGBT people make for particularly convenient targets. In Russia, it's especially so because it's a stand-in for many things at once. It's a way of saying, "If you want to go back to a past in which you felt more comfortable, before 1991, we just have to get rid of the gays," and the message is that there were no gay people in the Soviet Union. It's not a joke. There were no gay people in the Soviet Union. There were people who had sex with people of the same sex, and there were people who built all kinds of relationships, but there weren't people who claimed an identity and who claimed to belong to a group and who made rights claims based on belonging to a group. That was a distinct political phenomenon that occurred after the Soviet Union collapsed, and it was imported from the West, not because gay people were imported from the West but because these ideas were imported from the West. They were borrowed from cultures that had already formulated these ideas. So this was a way of saying if you want to get rid of everything that has made you uncomfortable in the past quarter century, and if you want to push back against the West, which wants to change our culture, wants to force their values down our throats, it's all about the gays. Another thing that makes the gays particularly convenient is that no Russian has ever knowingly met an LGBT person. Surveys bear this out. Maybe they've seen me on TV, or maybe they've seen this gay male performer, Boris Moiseev, but otherwise they've never actually met one in person. It is always more effective to scapegoat a minority that is not associated with people you know personally or members of your own family. Of course, in North America, we've known for a very long time that coming out

is key to social change, and over here I think we're witnessing a sort of milder version of the same thing, where Trump has reversed so many of the gains of the LGBT movement so fast, in part because it is the most recent and most rapid social change, so it very quickly communicates to his base that, Look, I'm taking you back to when America was great, and all the stuff that made you uncomfortable you no longer have to face, and look, I'm doing something because I'm reversing things that are signal achievements just of the past decade.

Wachtel: But as a result of that, you moved back to the United States with your family in 2013. You said you would have stayed in Moscow but for the safety of your children. How did it feel to emigrate to the U.S. a second time? Did you have a sense of defeat or of Putin winning?

Gessen: When my book about Putin came out in 2012 and I went on this very long international book tour, people would ask me, "How can you still live in Russia," and I would say, "Well, it's my home. He should go, and I'm staying." And it was a great line. It was an applause line, and now it's a laugh line. At the time, it gave me a sense of resolve, but he had the power. He had the monopoly on force, and when the state threatened quite transparently to go after my kids, we just packed up and left.

Wachtel: You identify now as non-binary in terms of gender, and this seems to have been a gradual process, initially driven by medical issues. What does it mean to you now? How much is being non-binary informed by your politics?

Gessen: You know, every time I write about this, I get into Twitter trouble, so I'm like a bad non-binary person. I wrote a big piece for the *New Yorker* on the hearings at the Supreme Court last month. It was amazing. So the Supreme Court heard arguments in the most consequential sexual-orientation and gender-identity discrimination case in its history, and all that the justices on both sides wanted to talk about was bathrooms. And the lawyers were saying, "No, it's not about the bathrooms. It's about employment discrimination." And the justices were literally saying, "Yes, but if we grant you this, they're going to want to go to the bathroom."

Wachtel: How did you get in trouble?

Gessen: I wrote this piece about how it's a three-hour hearing, and the justices keep talking about bathrooms, and finally I walk out of the hearing and realize I can't go to the bathroom. I can't go to the bathroom in this building, which is stupid because of course I could go to the bathroom in that building, but I felt like I couldn't, and I'd drunk two cups of coffee before the hearing. So I walked out onto the steps and there were Laverne Cox and Chase Strangio—Laverne is the transgender actress, and Chase is a transgender lawyer who's litigated several amazing cases; he's a young, brilliant lawyer—and they were both talking about going to the bathroom. Laverne said that she had gone to the women's room, and Chase said that he had gone to the men's room, and that he'd even gone in there with the Solicitor General, and I thought, I could've gone to the bathroom! So that was my last paragraph, and for that I got accused of being transphobic, and somehow that paragraph was interpreted as somewhat lording my non-binary identity over Chase's or Laverne's, or being resentful of their having gone to the bathroom—I was a little resentful that they had gone to the bathroom, but not in a political sense, more in a sort of physical sense.

But anyway, the reason I get in trouble is that I have written about the fact that I experience it very much as a choice, as a really exciting option that I'm exercising, and most of this work was not done by me this time. This political work done by transgender activists has made it possible to identify as a non-binary person, which is probably the most comfortable I've felt in my fifty-two years. But it's not something I knew I was going to do, say, a decade ago, and part of it had to do with a series of surgeries that I've had. This is the subject of another book that no one's ever read, called *Blood Matters*, about medical genetics, which I wrote after I found out I have the genetic mutation that is correlated with breast and ovarian cancer. It's recommended that women in that situation have all their female organs removed, so first I had a preventive mastectomy.

Wachtel: Your mother and her aunt . . .

Gessen: Women in my family died very early from these cancers, and the mutation is known. So I thought, Well, what would be a way of making lemonade out of these lemons, and I thought I could try being a dude or something, and I've written about that in some detail, and I think that some people perceive it . . . You know, for a lot of people, it's a lifelong struggle, and it's a sense of a deep inner need, and I can understand why my sometimes talking about it glibly or even talking about it as an option is offensive.

Wachtel: The day after the November 2016 election, you wrote in an article in the *New York Review of Books*, "Autocracy: Rules for Survival," that Donald

Trump was the first candidate in memory who ran not for president but for autocrat and won. Can you elaborate on that? You said the first rule is "believe the autocrat."

Gessen: I mean, some of that article sounds almost quaint now, but actually the story of that piece is kind of funny. So I was biking home from this disastrous election party—I think a lot of Americans have a memory from November 2016 of going to an election party and trying to disappear when it became clear which way things were going, and just leaving without saying goodbye to the hosts and trying to pretend it never happened—and I started getting phone calls and messages from friends asking, "What do we do now? What happens?" I thought, Why are you asking me? I'm living in exile; I obviously don't know how to deal with this. But then I thought, There has to be something I have learned over my nearly twenty years of covering Putin and Putinocracy, so I wrote this piece called "Autocracy: Rules for Survival," and I was supposed to file for the opinion pages of the *New York Times* that morning on Hillary's victory. They were so confident that they'd lined up all these people to write about their reactions to her victory all over the world, so I was supposed to write about the Russian reaction. They didn't really have anything of substance ready to go in case Trump won, and so I emailed the editor, saying, "How about I file this instead," and he said, "No, let's wait for the final results," and I'm like, "Come on, you know the results are final, but if you want I'll make it provisional." He said, "No, let's not."

So I sent it to the *New York Review of Books*, and they published it, and it's by far the most popular piece they've ever published. It crashed the site several times; it was pretty amazing. What I was pointing out about how Trump had run for autocrat had to do with the way he talked about power. People would focus on what he said about Putin: "He controls his country. You've got to give it to him. He's got control of the population." What was more interesting to me was the way he talked about power in that sentence. I think his admiration for Putin is actually quite genuine. It doesn't necessarily mean that Putin has something on him because Trump talks that way about every autocrat he encounters. His idea of power is control and unitary power, and power that's exercised performatively and constantly, and that's why I said he was running for autocrat.

Wachtel: What keeps you going? I say this in the context of this line that I have internalized, where you say, "Trumpian news has a way of being shocking without being surprising. . . . The difficulty with absorbing the news lies, in part, in the words we use, which have a way of rendering the outrageous ordinary." What keeps you going?

Gessen: I think I have a great gig. I have to write two columns a week for the *New Yorker*, so I can't ever get frustrated or angry about something for long; I just let off steam and keep going. It's a glib answer, but I feel so incredibly privileged to be able to write, and to feel like my words have some sort of impact and an audience, and to no longer be living in a country where nobody likes me. B̄

Sokrates to Krito (letter from prison)

ANNE CARSON

Dear Krito, don't come today. If you do, I'll have to pretend to be asleep or ashamed or explain why I sent my wife home. Tears are all about the weeper, aren't they? My kid has more sense. She was here, took one look around, said, *It's really damp in this place you need a hat*, came back a half-hour later with that woolly cap you gave me last winter. I like practical people. My death is set for three days hence. There's nothing you can do. But let me thank you for the hemlock. I know it wasn't cheap with the bribes and the tax—why can't they just grow the stuff in this country?—but God, it's better than the other way, the so-called bloodless crucifixion, with the stakes and the iron collar. No one wants to see another person die like that—Krito, you'd have nightmares for years. And I sort of like the idea of just numbing out. I've been numb for years, according to my wife—it was the only way to bear her—oh that was unkind. I've been unkind for years, at home anyway. Funny how the worst self comes out there. My life is guys, you know that! Guys and drinking. I'm a talker. I believe in talk—rip the lids off! let all the cats out of all the bags!—though most of what I say is just common sense. Do I frighten people? Claiming there's no back wall? Nothing between you and your heart of darkness? Or if there is, you can't pray to it, you can't write poems about it, you can't compete for its love. It smells of terrible plans and non-existence. Sorry, dramatic. Speaking of terrible plans though, don't let Plato visit me today either. He'll start quoting stuff I said in the old days, I shudder to hear it. Or he'll lecture me on The Law. *It's not the law putting you to death, it's the lawyers*, he'll say and I'll say, *Nice distinction*. Then he'll go on about swans or gymnastics or who knows what, he'll go on, go on, go on—whenever I talk to our dear Plato, I feel I'm drifting into eternity. You know what I mean. Or maybe you don't. You're an odd one, Krito. You look like Bob Dylan with your little gold eyes and your skinny arms. And you just love arguments, am I right? When did I stop caring about arguments? Because I did, I stopped. My mind is blank as bread. Maybe it's the hum in here. That humming, do you hear it? Is it in the walls or in my ears? Voices, voices, it's there all the time, voices with no words. It drowns out every other sound. Remember the old days when they'd play Iggy Pop all night to break the prisoners down? That was when the war was on; the beast is dozing now. Anyway, if you were here, I might not be able to get what you're saying—on the other hand, beloved Krito, if you do come, can you bring another one of those woolly caps? I gave mine to the guard. He looked miserable. It's really damp in this place.

For Toni Morrison

The following two pieces were among those read at a celebration of the life and work of Toni Morrison on November 21, 2019, at the Cathedral of St. John the Divine in New York City.

The Voice, the Craft
MICHAEL ONDAATJE

When has a voice been this intimate and versatile? Affectionate, far-reaching, self-aware, and also severe, dismissive of fools? There's that *range* in the manner of Toni Morrison's voice. She is always full of swerves—from humour, to anger, to music. We see all that in the narrator of *Jazz*, who holds this remarkable novel together.

"I like the feeling of a *told* story," Morrison has said, "where you hear a voice but you can't identify it. . . . It's a comfortable voice, and it's a guiding voice, and it's alarmed by the same things that the reader is alarmed by, and it doesn't know what's going to happen next either." Elsewhere, she writes, "To have the reader work *with* the author in the construction of the book—is what's important."

We are always participating when we read Toni Morrison. During a quiet lull, the narrator will remember: "And another damn thing!" Or in the middle of a flashback, she will parse a gesture: "That is what makes me worry about him. How he thinks first of his clothes, and not the woman. . . . But then he scrapes the mud from his Baltimore soles before he enters a cabin with a dirt floor and I don't hate him much anymore." It's those "Baltimore soles," and the precision of "*much* anymore." And besides, who else but Toni Morrison can interrupt a flashback? Her stories enact this constant switching of the formal and colloquial, of perspective and vocabulary, so that they feel gathered from everywhere. Where does this voice, this language, come from? Is it American Homeric?

There's a documentary on Charlie Parker that has a famous moment when he is asked what he thought set him apart from all the other saxophone players. His reply was simply, "The octave, man, just the octave."

"Do you have your audience in mind when you sit down to write?" Toni Morrison was once asked.

"Only me," she replied. I love the faith she has in her own craft. This is her talking to students in Mississippi:

> As I write I don't imagine a reader or listener, ever. I am the reader and the listener myself, and I think I am an excellent reader. I read very well. I mean I really know what's going on. . . . I have to assume that I am also this very critical, very fastidious, and not-easily-taken-in reader who is smart enough to participate in the text a lot.

And she speaks often of loving the rewrite: "The best part of it all, the absolutely most delicious part. . . . I try to make it look like I never touched it." This care for the gradually discovered story makes us fully trust her. It is how we are intimately altered by her books, and it was why *Beloved* would change everything.

I did get to meet and know Toni Morrison now and then, over the years, and what I remember most is her great humour. But I am really an intimate of hers *as a reader*. So I speak today as one of many writers—some of whom grew up in Pakistan, in Nigeria, Trinidad, Bogotá, or Tripoli—who love the skill of her craft, her moral voice. She is much more than "an American Writer." She is universal. Sometimes we find our true ancestors in other countries and become enlarged because we know their essays, their novels, those paragraphs that becalm us or devastate us, and so we no longer remain solitary in the distance.

I read *Jazz* for the first time in June of 1992, dazzled by its choreography: how she drew us with ease from 1926 Harlem back into the history of her characters; how she constructed and then reconsidered the story, until there was this fully lit diorama where we could witness the past while we remained in the intimacy of the present. All that done by the guiding voice of a narrator, who is, in a way, the most essential character in the book.

But here is the long-range octave, or what Morrison would call "the kick." Toward the end of *Jazz*, the narrator realizes that what is happening in the novel is not what she claimed so confidently would happen in the opening pages. She discovers, in fact, that there is more complexity in her invented characters than she imagined. And there is this moment when Morrison, in the voice of the narrator, allows her to confess to misinterpretation of those in the story:

> I missed the people altogether.
> . . . Now it's clear why they contradicted me at every turn: . . . they knew how little I could be counted on; how poorly, how shabbily my know-it-all self covered helplessness. That when I invented stories about them—and doing it seemed to me so fine— I was completely in their hands. . . .

So I missed it altogether. I was sure one would kill the other. I waited for it so I could describe it. I was so sure it would happen. That the past was an abused record with no choice but to repeat itself at the crack and no power on earth could lift the arm that held the needle.... I was the predictable one, confused in my solitude into arrogance....

. . . It never occurred to me that they were thinking other thoughts, feeling other feelings, putting their lives together in ways I never dreamed of.

It is this confession, made with craft and voice, that reveals the vast democracy of vision and humanity in Toni Morrison herself.

Hello Again, Ms. Morrison
EDWIDGE DANTICAT

I have been seeing you everywhere since you surrendered to the air and took your flight. I see you in bleak skies that are as "seductive as sunshine." I see you in daisy trees. I see you on benches by the road. I hear your voice in church hymns, spirituals, and jazz tunes because you were, as you wrote of Jadine in *Tar Baby*, "not only a woman but a sound," all the music we have ever wanted to play, as well as "a world, and a way of being in it."

I keep seeing you, too, in shiny, beautiful hairpins weaved through grey locks. Each time you gifted me one of those hairpins, I felt as though you were sharing pieces of your infinite crown with me. I still

February 13, 1974

Jill Krementz

feel your presence in your sister writer friends, in Sonia Sanchez and in Nikki Giovanni, and in my own writer sisters.

Though you carried a particular strand of genius in every single cell of your body, you constantly reminded us that it is indeed not scarce. This made it so much easier to tremble less in your presence. Because "quiet as it's kept," you half giggled when you laughed and you had a twinkle in your eye when you were in the presence of someone whose company you enjoyed. You drank vodka on a cold day—the really good stuff—and smoked cigarettes. At the Louvre. You were the literary giant that is Toni Morrison, but you were also Chloe Wofford, and you allowed me to see them both, for which I will always be grateful.

Your work, my goodness, the work is sublime. And we do not just read it, we experience it. You gave us both lullabies and battle cries. You turned pain into flesh and you brought spirits to life. You urged us to be dangerously free. You gave this foreigner a home.

Your work has carried me through adolescence and marriage, through parenthood and orphanhood. I have recited, and paraphrased, your sentences to myself while cradling the tiny bodies of my newborn daughters ("They get bigger, older, but grown? What's that suppose to mean?") and the skeletal faces of my dying parents. ("Soft as cream.") I hoped they would go soft as cream. And I came to think of you, as you wrote in *The Bluest Eye*, as "somebody with hands who does not want me to die."

"Death is as natural as life," you wrote. And you sure did live in this world!

Some of us called you Mother. Some of us called you Grandmother—Grand. Some of us called you Sister, Soror. Others called you Teacher, Editor, Mentor. We called you Our Beloved. Many in this room called you Friend, which is no casual title to you because friendship is a type of religion in your work, including friendships of the mind. We still call you by those names, but now we also call you Timeless. We now also call you Ancestor.

Standing here reminds me of that day in your home in Grand View, back in early 2016. We had spent the morning revisiting, for a documentary called *The Foreigner's Home*, the month you were in residence at the Louvre. We talked about slavery, racism, immigration, political art, Hurricane Katrina, breakdancing, and hip hop, particularly Kendrick Lamar. When it came time for me to leave, it was snowing outside and you were sitting by the window at your kitchen table with the winter afternoon light dancing across your face. I leaned down to kiss the top of your head, which was covered with a beautiful black-and-white scarf. In that moment I felt the sheer good fortune of already missing you long before you were gone.

My kiss on the top of your head created a spark that startled us both, with a surge of static electricity from the rug beneath our feet.

"Goodbye, Ms. Morrison," I said.

"Goodbye," you said, then you added, "I'm going to rest now."

"Dying was OK," you wrote, "because it was sleep."

In *Tar Baby*, a doubter is told, "The world will always be there—while you sleep it will be there."

This is true for you as well.

The world will be here, though certainly not as rich and not as full. It will still be here while you rest. And when you're done resting, remember, as another was also told through your voice, remember, "They are waiting in the hills for you. . . . the hills . . . where the . . . daisy trees still grow." They're waiting there for you. Your mother and your daddy, your beautiful son, Slade. Your sister, Lois. James Baldwin, Maya Angelou, Langston Hughes, Paule Marshall, Nina Simone, Billie Holiday, and so many others. They are all waiting in the hills for you. Go there and choose them, after your well-earned rest. B

What Stories Know about Us

JUAN GABRIEL VÁSQUEZ

I.

A year ago, almost to the day, my friend Enrique de Hériz—novelist, translator, clarinet player, amateur magician, knowledgeable sailor, and marathon runner—was diagnosed with lung cancer. He had been my only acquaintance when I arrived in Barcelona in October 1999 with one idea in my head: to earn a living from literature (whether reviewing, translating, or teaching it) while I dedicated every second of my waking life, including those spent earning a living, to the all-consuming task of becoming a novelist. I was twenty-six years old; at thirty-five, Enrique was much more than a host: he was a guide and an accomplice. He gave me and my wife a place to stay while we found something of our own; on his grandfather's desk, a massive beast that seemed to have occupied the same spot since the dawn of time, I wrote a short story that didn't make me blush: its title, "The All Saints' Day Lovers," would end up on the cover of my first acknowledged book. In the two decades that followed, Enrique became an unofficial godfather to my twin girls, and my wife and I became godparents to his children. We read each other's work and discussed the works of others, and prose fiction, every discovery and infatuation and corroboration and disappointment, was always at the centre of our talk, of our friendship, of our way of being in the world.

Last February, five months after the cancer diagnosis, I took two days off a scheduled trip to Lisbon to visit him in Barcelona. At the time, I was taking notes for this piece, trying to go deeper into my subject—indeed, trying to find what my subject was. During the past two years I had been obsessing about what I perceive to be the fundamental conflict of our times: what I have come to call "the breakup of the narrative contract." The narrative contract is an agreement that we understand reality through stories, and that even if stories contradict each other, we all accept that reality is still there: that there is such a thing as truth. Our narratives interpret truth differently because language contains or reflects experience, which is personal and unique like a fingerprint. But this has changed lately because truth is in crisis.

In 1964, Hannah Arendt published "Truth and Politics," a marvellous essay meant to confront "the enormous quantity of lies used in the controversy" that, years before, had surrounded *Eichmann in Jerusalem*. At some point in that essay, Arendt reflects on a quality of political thought she calls representative; that is, the fact that we form political opinions after consideration of several different points of view: those of people who are not here, whom we represent. She writes:

> This is a question neither of empathy, as though I tried to be or to feel like somebody else, nor of counting noses and joining a majority but of being and thinking in my own identity where actually I am not. The more people's standpoints I have present in my mind while I am pondering a given issue, and the better I can imagine how I would feel and think if I were in their place, the stronger will be my capacity for representative thinking and the more valid my final conclusions, my opinion.

I couldn't help noticing a kind of novelistic gesture in these words, even if the notion of empathy, which to me lives firmly at the centre of fiction as I understand it, was thoroughly dismissed by Arendt. Imagining how I would feel and think if I were in their place: isn't this precisely what fiction is about? Is it possible that there is an answer to be found in fiction, in the dedicated imagination of other people's lives, to the crisis of reality and truth? These were my thoughts as I arrived in Barcelona to visit Enrique.

I didn't go to see him right away. His daily routine, dominated by his illness, allowed for only a few minutes of social life in the afternoon. I walked around that city I knew well with a kind of anxiety I had never known before; Barcelona, in my mind, was inextricably linked to our friendship, and the boisterous city felt now strangely commanding, like the room next to which a patient is resting. As I climbed up the four flights of stairs to Enrique's apartment, wondering what I would find, I was aware of doing something that was already beyond his physical abilities. I knew he was not well. His chemo was not working; it had been replaced by immunotherapy, and now that wasn't working either. I knew all of this. But nothing could have prepared me for the brief conversation we had, whose import and density of meaning would only be apparent to me much later.

I asked him if he had any intention of writing about his illness. The question felt natural because this is what I would have done; but the way Enrique shook his head, in silent exhaustion, made me regret it. A chasm of experience had opened up between us, and his circumstances—his thoughts, his fears, his emotions—were for the first time out of my reach. He had become opaque. The conversation moved on and I asked him if he was working on a translation, even if only to keep busy. Didn't he have books to turn in? He said he had told his editors he would stop for a while. And this is when I asked him about his novel, the one he had been working on, the first pages of which I already knew and had discussed with him. In an email, he had written: "Among other things, the novel will investigate my very private obsession with voice (in a physical sense, but also in every symbolic sense). Voice as proof of life." It was now painful to hear his own voice, thinned down by the disease, tell me that he didn't plan to continue. His children were in their rooms and Yolanda, his wife, was fixing dinner, so I was alone with him when he looked me in the eye, with perfect awareness of what his words meant to me, and added, "I don't want any more stories."

Later I would realize, not without a sense of shame, that nothing had brought the truth home to me with such effectiveness as those words. I'd felt Enrique's depleted body when I embraced him; I'd seen this eloquent man reduce his conversation to its essentials because of shortness of breath. But only those words, *I don't want any more stories,* spoken with great effort in a voice that was definitely not a proof of life, carried with them the palpable possibility that a deeper transformation was taking place, that Enrique was turning away from life as we knew it. Because the mind of a reader often works in preposterous ways, I found myself abruptly remembering Joan Didion's volume of collected non-fiction: *We Tell Ourselves Stories in Order to Live.* Enrique, by his own account, had stopped telling stories to himself; he had also lost

the desire or the drive to tell them to the rest of us. No reader of fiction can entertain the illusion that we can fully know somebody else, whether it be our partners, our parents, or our friends. But this transformation seemed to me unlike any I had seen before: of a different order, and also of a different magnitude. Either my friend was becoming somebody else or he had ceased being the person whom I knew. It was also possible that I was reading too much into his words. Maybe, I thought as I walked down the stairs from his apartment, I was quite simply overblowing the metaphor.

I never saw Enrique again. Two weeks after my visit, he was admitted to the hospital with symptoms of severe asphyxia; one week after that, a mutual friend called me from Barcelona to let me know that Enrique was being sedated. That happened in the afternoon of Thursday, March 14, still morning in Colombia. I was working on this piece, taking notes about the political use of narrative, going back to my Orwell and my Arendt. That morning, as witnessed by my notebook, I was remembering the ominous epigram in *Nineteen Eighty-Four* that I have quoted so many times: "Who controls the past controls the future; who controls the present controls the past." I wanted to contrast those clairvoyant words with Arendt's reflections on political lies in general and the Pentagon Papers in particular, and I wanted to use these works to open my way into a reflection on the role of storytelling in the manufacturing, right here, right now, of a falsified reality. And there I was, looking at Winston Smith hard at work in the Ministry of Truth, distorting history and normalizing lies, when that same mutual friend called again to tell me that Enrique had stopped breathing.

The news of his death pushed me away from the desk, if for no other reason than because memories had started flooding in and I didn't want to think about anything else. (Deep sadness, of the kind you know you will only feel a few times in the course of a lifetime, is a selfish feeling.) What I did after a while was what I always do when writers die, if they have mattered to me: I take their books from my bookshelves and spend some time with them, browsing, looking at the words I have underlined in past readings, asking for quiet conversation. In one of my favourite poems, Francisco de Quevedo explained it well:

Withdrawn into the peace of this desert,
along with some books, few but wise,
I live in conversation with the deceased,
and listen to the dead with my eyes.

I sat down in my reading chair with Enrique's books around me, listening with my eyes to the voice of my friend, painfully realizing that he was, from now on, one of my dead. I opened his novel *Lies* and read the first few words, which I had known in manuscript fifteen years before and utterly forgotten.

"Dead?" says or writes his narrator. "Me, Isabel, dead? Not a chance. Not while I still have something to say about it."

There was an echo in those lines, an inverted rendition of the words I'd heard from Enrique's mouth: *I don't want any more stories*. I almost heard Enrique say, in flagrant contradiction of his narrator, "I have nothing else to say about it." *It* being, of course, life.

And this was problematic. No, not problematic: that contrast between the exhausted voice of my friend and the vitality of his character's became to me nothing short of haunting. Isabel is a woman in her sixties who has been declared dead while she's alive and well in the Guatemalan jungle; telling her story will be the way to claim control over her life, to come back to life. Enrique, at fifty-five, had devoted his whole adult life to fiction, as a novelist or an editor or a translator or a reviewer, and at some point had decided to renounce—at least in my interpretation of his words—everything that his life had been about. That's what he was when I last saw him: a man in retreat from himself. *I don't want any more stories.*

I discovered that attempting to understand exactly this, the place within my friend where these words came from, allowed me a kind of sustained contact with his memory; most importantly, the effort seemed to address meaningful issues for me, although I wouldn't have been able to name what they were. In other words, I realized I was trying to find an answer but had not been able to formulate the question.

I took the notes I'd been scribbling for this piece and set them quietly aside. I returned those books to their bookshelves. And then I started writing the pages you have just read.

II.

It's quite likely that the reason I was so bothered by Enrique's words was that they questioned, or rather confronted, some assumptions that have informed my life as a novelist. You see, fiction, at its core, has always seemed to me one of the most forceful rebuttals of death we human beings have come up with. Joan Didion's title feels accurate for any serious reader of fiction, but what does it ultimately mean? Perhaps that we always want to say more. To tell stories (about ourselves, about others) is to be entrenched in life, indisputably a part of it; at the simplest level, an appetite for stories means an appetite for life: the testimony that we still have something to say about it. Yes, that's what it is: voice as a proof of life.

We also read and write stories because life, as bestowed on us, fails to satisfy us. I want to live more lives, we say. I want to know more things. Life's fundamental limitations are twofold: we only have one, meaning that it ends with biological death; and we only have one, meaning that we are trapped in a single experience, a single set of existential coordinates. There is little or nothing I can do to change the fact that I am male, white, and forty-six years old. Reading fiction, however, I have come reasonably close to *being* (I make good use of my italics here) a Latin American dictator in his old age, a Russian student who is a murderer, a black woman who is a slave, a teenage girl of French descent who discovers sex in Asia, a teenage boy of Jewish descent who discovers sex in New Jersey, an orphan growing up in sixteenth-century Spain, an orphan growing up in nineteenth-century London, a German poet, a German war criminal, a man who turns into vermin, a man who turns into a nose, a man who turns into a Mexican fish, a Mexican fetus who has not been born, a Roman soldier who will never die.

I am grateful to James Wood for calling my attention to these words of George Eliot: "Art is the nearest thing to life; it is a mode of amplifying experience and extending our contact with our fellow-men beyond the bounds of our personal lot." That amplification

© Jacques Oulé

of experience, that extension of human contact, is not unique to narrative fiction, but it always requires two components without which narrative fiction is unable to illuminate or discover anything: observation and imagination. "One must paint the peasants as if one were one of them, feeling, thinking as they do themselves," said Vincent van Gogh, probably discussing *The Angelus* he painted after Millet in 1880. Feeling and thinking as somebody else, of course, is best achieved after watching them closely. Van Gogh could do it, and Caravaggio before him, and Lucian Freud after him. Their powers of observation are of the same nature as those of Chekhov or Joyce or Proust, or Toni Morrison or Javier Marías or Alice Munro, but the way we inhabit their creations is different *because fiction is made of language.*

Take, for instance, the opening of *Anna Karenina*: "All happy families are alike; each unhappy family is unhappy in its own way." I would submit to you that no two readers share an identical definition of what a family is, let alone what happiness or unhappiness is or feels like. When we read Tolstoy's words, we fill them with our own private experience, our memories (suppressed or not), our idiosyncrasies (hidden or apparent), our intuitions of the inner workings of human beings. Words are vessels; we pour our humanity into them; but, since they are being used in a context, since they come to us charged with their own knowledge and experience—the meaning that those words, *family* and *happiness* and *unhappiness*, have for the Oblonskys—our intimate understanding is enlarged. Of course, by the time the novel ends, none of the Oblonskys will have the same relationship with those words. Those words will have changed painfully for the Karenins as well as for Vronsky; they will have changed for the reader. We feel we know more things; we feel we have lived more lives. This is probably why we sense, when reading great fiction, that the words know more about us than we do: that the novel is reading us.

The same phenomenon is probably familiar to most writers. We know that Tolstoy began writing *Anna Karenina* with the idea of a fallen woman whose suicide was the necessary punishment for her adultery. His very first idea, as expressed in 1870 to his wife, was about a woman more pitiful than guilty. But his moral stance changes when he begins writing; in the early drafts, Anna was vulgar and unattractive and her husband was smart, humble, a true representative of Christian values. As the novel progressed, Anna grew in complexity, depth, and even beauty, while her husband became petty, insincere, a slave to the hypocrisy of others. The novel began exploring the hidden aspects of human behaviour—its contradictions, its mysteries—transcending the social commentary or moral fable that it started out to be and complicating Tolstoy's rather simple premise. This is probably what Milan Kundera means when he says that novels are more intelligent than their authors. Failed novels, I've always felt without a single shred of evidence, are written by novelists who always know more than their stories, who are always one step ahead. The task of the novelist, in this sense, would be to find a form—in style and architecture—that allows the novel to think for itself, to explore places the novelist wouldn't have dared to visit or maybe didn't even know existed.

Nabokov famously mocked the impulse we have, as readers, to identify with fictional characters: his was the elegant cynicism of an aesthete. I've always suspected this refusal is at the root of his inability to fully appreciate Miguel de Cervantes or Fyodor Dostoevsky. When he disparages *Don Quixote* as primitive, when he calls Dostoevsky mediocre and sentimental, he is fundamentally accusing them of not caring enough about form. And, yes, there's no baggy monster as loose as Cervantes's novel; and *Crime and Punishment* proclaims on every page the fact that it was dictated, rather than composed, by a novelist drowning in debt and unable to rewrite or reconsider. But I would be hard-pressed to think of a writer as generous or compassionate as Cervantes, capable of penetrating the moral realities of just about everyone his knight encounters in his quest: a female shepherd, a captive soldier, a university student, a puppet master who is a con artist. And if being sentimental and mediocre won't impede a legacy that includes the Underground Man or Alyosha Karamazov, then I would like to sign up to that club with no further delay. Nabokov constantly censures Dostoevsky for not clearly seeing either his scenes or his characters. There's a moment in Nabokov's *Lectures on Russian Literature* where he draws a sketch of the sleeping car in which Anna Karenina is travelling from Moscow to Saint Petersburg; nothing of the sort could be done with, for instance, the place where Stavrogin meets the bishop Tikhon in *Demons*. It is true that we don't usually know what precisely Dostoevsky's characters are wearing, but nothing of their hearts and minds escapes us. No moral or emotional stone is left unturned, and it's a dangerous exploration, for Dostoevsky opens his eyes where the rest of us would have rather closed them.

There's a wonderful documentary about Svetlana Geier, Dostoevsky's translator into German. She calls his great novels "The Five Elephants." I will dare any reader to take a ride on them, one after the other, and hop down without feeling that their life is utterly transformed. "One doesn't translate this with impunity," Geier says, pointing at the five published monsters she has authored. I can assure you no one reads them with impunity either.

It's this inhabiting of another's existential coordinates, this metaphysical sleight of hand, where we find some of the greatest satisfactions (and the most urgent assistance) that fiction is able to provide. And although the magic, admittedly, doesn't always happen, it is still true that in the care of a certain kind of writer we occupy someone else's consciousness, and dwell in it, in a way that is nothing short of supernatural. Perhaps this is as useful a yardstick as any other: literary greatness measured by the depth and richness with which a writer's language enlarges our sense of the human, pushing back the limits of what can be felt and thought, discovering new territories. Henry Fielding remembers somewhere that the Latin word *inventio*, in its etymology, means "to discover." Fiction discovers: the past, in Proust or Marguerite Yourcenar; the present, in Joyce or Woolf; the future, in Orwell or Atwood. Without García Márquez or Borges, whole territories of the human experience would be unavailable to us. In a sense, what we call human experience is the summation of our stories, the stories we tell, whether they are made up or not. But when one of those experiences is important and it has been fixed in a durable form, both beautiful and efficient in language, structure, and dramaturgy, fully observed and adroitly imagined, we the readers feel that, as Adolfo Bioy Casares fittingly put it, a room has been added to the house of life.

We read fiction because we are thirsty for knowledge of a particular kind that we can't get elsewhere. Or, should I say with a little hubris, that only happens in imaginative writing: the things we learn in fiction can only be found there. *The Myth of Sisyphus*, Camus's philosophical essay about the concept of the absurd, doesn't offer us the same kind of information that is to be found in *The Stranger*, which is usually taken to be a narrative discussion of the same themes. But

© Jacques Oulé

fiction is never about one thing only; its concerns, because of the way imaginative prose goes about its business, are ambiguous and often contradictory. We read *The Stranger* because it satisfies different curiosities than *The Myth of Sisyphus*. Meursault's story speaks to a different part of what we are as human beings, among other reasons because it is Meursault's story, not Camus's meditations. Most importantly, because where the philosophical essay tries to provide an answer to difficult questions, the novel is reticent: it denies the reader any kind of definitive resolution. Why did Meursault kill the Arab? We'll never know; but it is through that withheld motive that the novel says what it has to say. Why was Joseph K. arrested? We'll never know; but if Kafka had given us an answer—shoplifting, say, or possession of pornography—*The Trial* would not be the visionary fiction it is, capable of discovering a new world, so distinctive and necessary that we had to invent an adjective: Kafkaesque. If we had that little piece of useful information, *The Trial* wouldn't read today as a port of entry to an undiscovered country but merely—and woefully—as a very weird version of *Les Misérables*.

This is what the Spanish novelist Javier Cercas, in a superb book of essays, calls "the blind spot" of the novel. The expression comes from a place in our optic disc that lacks light detectors; no image can therefore be seen there. Since the blind spots of our two eyes don't coincide, one eye sees what the other doesn't, and we remain unaware of this blindness; but what matters most for our purposes is that the human brain, gathering the available information, is able to, as it were, fill in the blanks. For Cercas, this ophthalmological curiosity amounts to a metaphor of what novels are and of how they work, or at least a certain family of novels toward which he feels a particular attachment. There is a spot in the novel's eye where nothing can be seen: we don't know what crime Joseph K. committed; we don't know why Meursault kills the Arab. But it is precisely through that blindness that the novel is able to see; it is through that silence that the novel speaks. At the heart of these novels, Cercas writes,

> there is a question, and the whole novel consists of a search for an answer to this central question; when this search is finished, however, the answer is that there is no answer, that is, the answer is the search itself, the question itself, the book itself. In other words: in the end there is no clear, unequivocal, emphatic answer; only an ambiguous, equivocal, contradictory, essentially ironic answer, which doesn't even resemble an answer.

On my copy of Cercas's book, after my first reading, I transcribed these words from a letter Chekhov wrote to Alexei Suvorin in 1888: "You are right to demand that an author take conscious stock of what he is doing, but you are confusing two concepts: *answering the questions* and *formulating them correctly*."

One of the stories Cercas discusses, albeit briefly, as an example of the blind spot is *Bartleby, the Scrivener*:

> We will never know the truth of who this man is or what he represents, this man who has no family and speaks only to reply and never goes outside and spends his time off staring blankly at a blank wall and nobody knows where he came from or where he's going; we'll never know why his soul is sick or what kind of illness he suffers from or why he is "the saddest of men"; we'll never know whether he's absolutely mad or totally sane, or if he's the very personification of rebellion or of conformity.

Melville's long short story, that cryptic masterpiece of melancholy, has always been a favourite of mine, and I have always read it with as much admiration as uncertainty; but earlier this year it gained an altogether new pertinence in my life. The following rationalization is imperfect, but it is the only one I can give right now.

III.

A week or so after my visit to Enrique, our mutual friend, the publisher Pere Sureda, called me with a proposal of sorts. For several years he had been commissioning new translations of significant books from his closest collaborators; he had published my translation of Conrad's *Heart of Darkness*, for instance, and Enrique had translated several books for him. Over the phone he told me something that Enrique had withheld from me: that he had turned in his most recent commission a couple of months ago but had not been able to revise it, out of physical and intellectual fatigue, and was unwilling to let anybody else do it: he loved that story too much. The book—for it would be published as an independent volume—was *Bartleby, the Scrivener*. "You're the only person he would suffer to touch his work," Pere said to me. And this was his proposal: that I revise Enrique's translation and write a preface in as short a time as possible, so that the book could be hurried to press and presented to our friend as a gift. The implications were clear: he didn't think Enrique had long to live.

With that in mind I read *Bartleby* again, maybe for the tenth time in my life. And for the eleventh time too: because first I went through Melville's words and then over Enrique's Spanish version, as moving and precise as the original. Now, one of the most bewildering properties of great fiction—also of great poetry—is that it changes as we change: whoever reads *The Divine Comedy* at twenty and then at forty will read two different, almost incompatible books. In *A History of Reading*, Alberto Manguel remembers what Woolf says in an essay about Charlotte Brontë: that reading *Hamlet* every year and writing down our impressions is almost like writing our autobiography; for as we live on, we discover that Shakespeare also talks about what we have just learned. So yes: it was predictable that *Bartleby* should have changed for me too. But will you believe me (no, will you forgive me) if I confess that I wasn't quite aware, until the very last minute, of the nature of that change? The story of the clerk who refuses to write spoke to me in different ways this time around, not only because the words I was reading had been chosen, every single one of them, by Enrique de Hériz but also because Bartleby's reply, the all-too-famous "I would prefer not to," had become a chamber in which another reply, disquieting, uncomfortable, could be heard: "I don't want any more stories." Reading fiction entails risks because our deepest emotions are always in play, ready to surface, the language becoming emotionally charged, capable of reaching into hidden or forgotten regions of our consciousness. In a way, it was Enrique's voice, broken by cancer, that I was hearing now over Bartleby's words. I felt as close to the narrator as I could ever be, both inquiring into the mystery of another.

On the last page of the story, Bartleby has already died and been buried. The lawyer-narrator declares his curiosity for the enigmatic man and for his enigmatic past; that curiosity, he says, he is unable to satisfy. And yet he feels the need to share with us a rumour that has contained for him "a certain strange suggestive interest." Apparently, Bartleby used to work as a clerk in the Dead Letter Office, whose task is to sort and finally burn the missives that never reach their destinations. "Sometimes," he reflects,

from out the folded paper the pale clerk takes a ring:—the finger it was meant for, perhaps, moulders in the grave; a bank note sent in swiftest charity:—he whom it would relieve, nor eats nor hungers any more; pardon for those who died despairing; hope for those who died unhoping; good tidings for those who died stifled by unrelieved calamities. On errands of life, these letters speed to death.

The narrator finds something illuminating in that discovery. I do too. The narrator is unable to put his finger exactly on what that discovery illuminates. So am I. A kind of consolation is all I can get from the words of Melville, which are also my friend's words.

And it is quite enough. 🅱

Bo Huston, Forgotten

JOHN MCINTYRE

I know that death is merely a rumor. I pay it no mind. Disappearance is the real dilemma.
— Bo Huston

In the final years of his life—a cruel phrase, really, as he only lived to thirty-three—the writer Bo Huston made several trips to Zurich for experimental AIDS treatments. In his downtime there, between appointments, he read Christopher Isherwood and Patricia Highsmith, slept, and went for walks to fill the days.

Huston had left Ohio years earlier for Hampshire College in Massachusetts, but the New York demimonde of nightclubs and public baths, the random assignations, and the louche and fearless personas men honed in pursuit of them was irresistible. He enrolled in film school at New York University in the early 1980s, that most consequential decade for the community he found a home in, and took up work as a typesetter. It was also in New York that he became addicted to heroin, and he left the city for Rhinebeck, New York, with hopes of kicking the habit. He left the East Coast for good in 1987 for San Francisco. In 1988 he was diagnosed as being HIV positive, and he resigned from his job in advertising, an event that set in motion his life as a writer.

From the time of HIV's appearance to the end of 1988, more than eighty-two thousand cases were reported in the United States. Of those eighty-two thousand individuals diagnosed, more than sixty-one thousand had died. Huston might've assumed a one-in-four chance of living with HIV. But even those odds reflected a best-case scenario of five years. At a Christmas party the previous year, he'd met the man of his life, Dan Carmell. "Dan, by his presence, confirms my presence," Huston wrote prior to his death. "My alliance and exchanges with Dan complete my picture of myself." The following June, the year of his diagnosis, he had his twenty-ninth birthday.

AIDS represents a pervasive sense of urgency in my life: if I am terminal, if my time is limited, if my competence, longings, affections, motivation are all unpredictable, I push harder. I want my book published now, *before I am too weak to read. I want to paint my apartment* now, *while I can still balance on a ladder. I want sex with some cute guy* today, *before this pastime has left the realm of my desires. Ironically, two books are done, the apartment is gleaming white, I cannot possibly count the nameless trysts . . . and I'm still here, still racing.*

Huston wasn't the first writer to hear he was unlikely to live long enough to finish his work. He wasn't even the first writer of his generation, or his circle of friends. If he'd looked to the past for examples, there was the English writer Anthony Burgess, who famously received a brain-tumour diagnosis at forty and was told he had a year to live. Burgess set to writing, intent on leaving something to support his wife and children. The resulting manuscripts—five novels' worth, including one entitled *The Doctor Is Sick*—formed the foundation of his career as a writer. But Burgess far outlived his doctor's prognosis, dying at seventy-six.

At the time of his diagnosis, Huston had published film reviews and short fiction, but his first book, *Horse and Other Stories*, didn't appear until 1989. His early work established his affinity for lyrical, compressed stories about young, gay men making lives for themselves in the face of familial and societal pressures. His second book, a novel called *Remember Me*, appeared in 1991, and another novel, *The Dream Life*, followed in 1992. A fourth and final book, *The Listener*, was published the year after his death. Four books in five years, and work left unfinished. In an interview with Andréa R. Vaucher, Huston said, "My main resentment about working and starting to get published and successful and having AIDS, has been the fear that I'm not going to get to mature as a writer."

However, Huston found one of his work's recurring concerns in living with AIDS. It's possible he felt

like the writer Andrew Holleran, who notes in his 1987 essay "Reading and Writing" that "I was so worried that the subject would repel readers (I still assume this, since I, too, am a reader and that is my reaction) that I discussed it only when I had to; eventually, just as the dictatorial cruelty of AIDS touched everything, it seemed I had to, all the time." Yet Huston couldn't, and didn't, share Holleran's sense that "Literature could not heal or explain this catastrophe. . . . Novels weren't needed. . . . To attempt to imagine such scenes seemed impertinence of the worst kind."

Huston had remarked that he'd be thrilled to be known in fifty years' time as a minor gay writer from the 1990s. He'd shown promise and at times something finer, a light touch, a talent for crafting memorable sentences, and a sophisticated grasp of the relationships that occupy the centre of our lives. Extravagant claims for his work won't stand up, but he wrote far too well for us to dismiss him altogether.

Someone asks, what is your novel about? Togetherness, I answer.

You could argue that *Remember Me* is one of the "tentative first novels from defunct presses" that Sarah Schulman calls an artifact of the years predating antiretroviral treatments in her book *The Gentrification of the Mind*. It's a dark novel, inward-looking, and perhaps unbalanced, in that it's short on the anger and outrage that also attended the losses of those years. The reviews upon its release were unenthusiastic. Huston took the book's reception badly, and perhaps he had a legitimate gripe. One of the most prominent notices, in *Publishers Weekly*, took time out of a capsule treatment to note that "the narrator graphically describes his anonymous homosexual encounters, including a visit to a 'porno place,'" which seems a demerit in the writer's estimation and exaggerates the book's sexual content besides.

Remember Me is a slim, lyrical novel set in a fictionalized Rhinebeck, New York, though Huston offers so few particulars that the setting could as easily be a provincial town in France. "This town is nestled between two small hills along the river," Huston writes. "Patches of green and brown are threaded by the railroad tracks. The tiny houses, a steeple, a train station, a whitewashed flagpole in its center make it seem like a toy town that one need not take too seriously."

The unnamed narrator and his friend Charlotte have static lives, a static life together. They've known each other since childhood, and she nurses the scars on her legs from burns that were the narrator's fault years earlier. This, plus her psychic aversion to dealing with the outside world—the noise and motion, the unfamiliar people—consigns her to day upon day at home, working on her "projects." She bounces from poetry to short stories to collage, completing nothing she undertakes.

The narrator fares better in his attempts as a writer, but the small press interested in his novel goes out of business before he's completed their recommended edits. Like Charlotte, he's locked within himself by a mixture of personality, experience, and, in his case, socially stigmatized illness. He's profoundly isolated, has almost no physical contact, even in memory. He

has little emotional connection either, apart from Charlotte and their codependent bond.

For all the darkness, though, and all the stasis, there's something seductive about the voice, style, and slant of the narrator's mind. The prose has the cadence of an elegant translation, the directness and definite pronouncements one might find in Marguerite Duras. And it is a translation of sorts, of the spectre of death, filtered through the sensibility of a young and previously healthy individual. The narrator's illness is more a looming dread than a conglomeration of symptoms. When he has a serious health scare late in the novel, a sudden fever brought on by an infection that lands him in the hospital for several days, the episode reads as a sharp increase in the threat level he faces.

Remember Me is part of the mosaic of literary responses to the HIV/AIDS epidemic, one worthy of a place of honour. So many of those books are forgotten now—the carefully honed stories of Allen Barnett's *The Body and Its Dangers*, a virtuoso performance that was both a debut and farewell. Christopher Coe's *Such Times*, which makes an anonymous hand job in its latter stages both elegiac and valedictory. The soaring romanticism of Robert Ferro's *Second Son*, in which Mark Valerian, the second son of a large family, unexpectedly falls in love while both he and his new partner attempt to manage the same life-threatening illness. Ferro forgoes mention of AIDS entirely, "for fear," as Holleran recalls, "of letting this virus reduce his writing, too, to an aspect of the plague." James McCourt's *Time Remaining*, which the writer Michael LaPointe said in a 2018 *New Yorker* piece "glimmers heroically" in its portrayal of the irreverence and resilience of a pair of drag queens (Miss Mae Mae and Odette O'Doyle) coping with the loss of all the other members of their troupe. Other books remain in print: Allan Gurganus's *Plays Well with Others*, its humour balanced so deftly against racking loss, its protagonist, Richard Hartley Mims Jr., seeking solace in isolation, having moved back to North Carolina and away from all the pain he'd experienced in New York. And there's Felice Picano's *Like People in History*, with its large canvas and delicate weave of events, following a pair of cousins as they live through everything from the repression of the 1950s to the free-for-all of Fire Island in the 1970s and the urgency of AIDS Coalition to Unleash Power (ACT UP)–style activism, which anchors a significant scene in the novel. These books and others like them form a multifaceted picture of the pain, loss, and waste of those early years of the plague and of the impossible pressures and constraints facing writers who responded to the crisis in real time.

As for Huston, he wrote to the end, or as close as he could get to it. Thomas Avena recounts their final phone exchange in his introductory essay to *Life Sentences*. "I won't be around much longer," Huston tells him and says they should finish their edits. "I said that I had always admired him," Avena writes, "that his last novel, *The Dream Life*, was a perfect work, seamless. . . . We went carefully over the edits."

The Dream Life remains in print. It's the only one of Huston's books that is, although there's a viable case to be made for reprinting each of the three out-of-print titles. Yet Huston's fondest wish has come true: his books are available in libraries in the U.S. and abroad. It's gratifying to think that, like *Remember Me*'s unnamed narrator writing his novel about togetherness, Huston can be together with readers more than a quarter-century after his death. Those who encounter his work today may be unable to remember him—much of his generation, sadly and unjustly, is already gone—but it's not hard to imagine a young, hungry writer feasting on his books, wondering what might have been while savouring the writing Huston left behind.   B̄

The Future Accidental

ROB WINGER

© Ken Babstock

Poetry has that ability to reconstitute language; it uses time. It can make you see the xylem between the then and the after, or the now and the after. It has no obligation to the present. It is time.

— Dionne Brand

At a tiny farm-to-table restaurant on Ossington Avenue, I lean over my cherry flan. It's the end of the meal. I've already eaten most of my whipped cream. Across from me, my friend remains phoneless and much smarter than I'll ever be. She insists not on a personal resistance to technology but instead on a refusal to be dictated by it. "I'll be out to dinner with eight friends," she says, "and fully half will be looking down, like this." Under the table, she holds her palm flat and stares at it. And she clarifies: it's not *affect* but *effect*—the way our lives adjust to technology until that technology reshapes how we organize our lives. The way, at Angkor Wat one morning five years ago, she says, each person around her privileged the machines in their pockets, not the ones behind tissue and bone, holding up their screens between their faces and each relief sculpture lit by the vital, irreplaceable Siem Reap dawn.

Susan Sontag seems already to have understood this almost forty years ago. In *On Photography*, she postulates that then-contemporary 1970s tourist picture-taking is really an extension of capital, an activity that allows those ensnared in the economies of market exploitation to rationalize the utility of a break from the grind without feeling too bad about taking a holiday. My friend and I both know this. Either one of us might quote Georg Simmel's 1903 essay "The Metropolis and Mental Life," which claims that modern urban reality allows for both a sense of "personal freedom" and a simultaneous suspicion that each of us is just "a mere cog in an enormous organization of things and powers." Or we might recall a seemingly opposite impulse from the same era: John Muir, treed in his nineteenth-century California redwoods, glorying in the salve of electricity-free natural spaces. Both postures, it seems to me, reflect a historically consistent way of being in the world that many of us tend to misread as uniquely, grotesquely present tense.

"I'm always suspicious," I say, our dessert nearly done, "of the idea that anything is really new."

Right now, almost all of us have phones in our pockets. So almost all of us carry a full library that's accessible with a search bar and the means to access and pay a cellular bill; there, on our pocketed screens, is the capacity to produce more images in a single day than could be created in a decade a hundred years ago; there we find satellite access to eons of pixelated maps we now routinely use to navigate new cities or subway lines. Does this mean that the digital age, the social-media age, the present age is in any way fundamentally different than what preceded it? Does the invention of the cellphone and the internet constitute a wholly new kind of human experience, as we're so often told it does? And what do we mean when we say the word *new* anyhow?

In almost any decade within the past two centuries, after all, one can almost always, with accuracy, make these sorts of statements: the human race has never gone as fast as it's going now; we've never wrecked so much so quickly; we've never created or seen so many images; we've never been closer to living in a single social village; we've never seen such violence; the world has never been so small. In his easy 1850s New England cabin, Henry David Thoreau seemed to confirm this sort of present-tense exceptionalism. He famously dismissed daily newspaper reportage by claiming, in *Walden*, both that "To a philosopher, all *news*, as it is called, is gossip" and that he "could easily do without the post-office"; both statements react to the invasion by the 1840s of daily newspapers into everyday American life. To Thoreau, newspaper news simply increased the volume, traffic, and scale of all the junk already circulating.

"So," my friend says across the table, "maybe the question is about urgency, not singularity." Maybe when we say "new" we're talking about energy, not a collapsing or dividing of history into tidy eras such as The Past and The Present. Maybe we're talking about a feeling or a condition, not an era or an absolute.

Purists like Thoreau were supposedly appalled with people in mid-century cafés placing between themselves and their companions giant sheaves of newsprint, thereby allowing technology—since even a paper or a book is a form of technology—to interrupt otherwise engaged, face-to-face exchanges. While different in speed and volume than contemporary digital sources, nineteenth-century newspapers were anchored by an algorithmic market economy—they only stayed in business by successfully targeting ads to their audiences. To me, Thoreau's critiques sound a whole lot like what Cal Newport calls the vital need for "digital minimalism," which advises us to save ourselves from dopamine-releasing clickbait addictions, fears of missing out, or nagging urges to frame and regulate our lives online. That urge to check, post, and update also echoes the way Sontag's tourists documented their hikes to the edge of the Grand Canyon: both tasks can feel like work rather than play.

What then, if anything, marks our time, here and now, as unique? And is the implicit quest for novelty even the right thing to be thinking about? Does any urge to say our time is different or more complex than the supposedly "simpler" times that came before reveal a narrowness similar to the egotistical branding demanded by most social-media platforms? And, if so, what does this say about my own attempts to focus on what's new? Is Thoreau really right that the only news is the kind that lasts?

Here are some lines written by one of my literary heroes, American poet Adrienne Rich, way back in the early 1990s, nearly thirty years ago—lines I read on a commuter train on my way to see my friend at this table where we're now sitting—that conclude the horror-filled, beautiful title sequence of her book, *An Atlas of the Difficult World*:

> I know you are reading this poem listening for
>   something, torn
>   between bitterness and hope
> turning back once again to the task you
>   cannot refuse.
> I know you are reading this poem because
>   there is nothing else

> left to read
> there where you have landed, stripped
>   as you are.

How is it possible that such lines remain fully contemporary? How is it possible for Rich's decades-old stanzas to speak so precisely about all the seemingly new versions of populism rising around the world right now? The answer, I think, cannot simply involve myths of genius or artistic immortality. As Rich's American contemporary Kurt Vonnegut noted, promoting such familiar tropes would probably just be "show business."

The answer, instead, seems to involve establishing situation and context, then sharing with sureness any possible faith in provisional knowledge; that's what happens, for me, in the best moments of the best kinds of reading or writing. In our current era—as long as what we say is not extremist, hateful, fundamentalist, ill-informed, or functionally closed—to declare anything with certainty is a revolutionary act. It is no longer rebellious or novel to point out all the tiny ways in which what we think we know cannot possibly be absolute. Instead, it's a revolution to locate with poetic precision, as Rich so often does, one boat on one sea, one wreck accessed by one ladder that leads down into a single, singular ocean. It's a revolution to declare we know any answers.

All of us who are at least partially awake to the state of the twenty-first-century world recognize the ebb and flow that Rich locates in the lines above: we're "torn," she writes, "between bitterness and hope." And, sadly, this is not news, especially given the ways that the ugliest parts of populism continue to shape the cultural realities of so many who can't claim the privileged qualifiers I was able, for so long, to ignore: middle class, cishet, white, male. Perhaps binaries such as "bitterness and hope," as I read them, are therefore foundational; they certainly feel like primary elements in Ecclesiastes or the Tao Te Ching or the Dhammapada. What's *new*, maybe, in the sense Thoreau might have meant it, is the constant newness reactivated when we read lines that cheat or complicate time, that clarify our present conditions without any need for definitive historical footnotes. What's new is our apprehension, over and over, of lines floated forward to us as so many proverbial bottled messages.

When I uncork a line in a novel or poem that accomplishes this sense of revolutionary newness—a newness that risks saying it might know, despite all the evidence that reminds us that we can't quite know—I react less with my scholarly training or aesthetic judgment than I do with my body. I react involuntarily. When I read such lines, such as the immaculate conclusion to Toni Morrison's novel *Song of Solomon*, or the final stanzas of Pablo Neruda's "Ode to the Onion," or the best poems of Adrienne Rich, this is what happens: the hairs on my arms and on the back of my neck stand on end, my body shivers, there's a drop in my stomach as though I'm descending a small hill at top speed in a car on a country road, my eyes well up, my throat swells and chokes, I can't speak. Something breaks and is healed all at once.

The way I respond to the world is informed by my knowledge of this place, which simultaneously allows for an intuitive bodily reaction and an intellectual recognition of declaration as revolutionary risk. Is this response influenced by technological newness, or by the ways we might be shaped by social media, or by the necessity to accelerate into digital all the processes so many of us first learned in analog? Does it make any sense to mourn the loss of the latency between exposing a negative image on film and witnessing its positive results on paper? I'm thinking about these questions at the table, where my friend still holds her palm flat, trying to understand what's new, if anything, in how all of us are formulating and engaging with and disconnecting from the worlds around us.

Those of us who read and write poetry—regardless of whether it's performative or conceptual or lyrical and on the page—are answering these questions when we use language that doesn't pretend, that rejects the fashionable or polite, that declares the weird truths it sees. And such truths can't be simplified into any sort of slogan, wherein sure declaration equals new knowledge equals safe beauty. Rather than simply adopting Ezra Pound's old "make it new" mantra—advice so often twisted in the past century into formulations that translate as "make it *look* new" or "make it *seem* new"—such declarations perhaps involve responding with both artistic integrity and ethical honesty to whatever we find around us.

Moral and political responses to the awful public hatefulness of right-wing populism are required not only in poetry, of course, but also in real-life conversations and contexts. The left, for all its excellent intentions, tends to imitate the machinations of the right on social media, speaking directly to its own constituents in its own language to villainize and dehumanize its own targets. That I agree with the moral assumptions of those who engage in such targeting is troubling to me. But I worry that something like writing a poem is a similar retreat, a movement back into silo-thinking, into choir-preaching, into the ease of beauty. Is Phyllis Webb still right, then, that "the proper response to a poem is another poem"?

To think about this question, I'm trying to understand the urgencies of the now without simply dividing history into a tidy before-and-after, a misleading this-and-only-this. I'm testing what might be new in what we like to call "our time." Are the ways we pose for a coiffed selfie essentially any different than the ways we've always put on fashionable masks to enact public versions of ourselves? And can't an insistence on truth-telling also be a game, a ruse, a limitation, a humblebrag? Has our era's demand always to respond, always like, always showcase our daily lives truly reshaped how we apprehend, understand, and translate the world? I'm unsure. It seems possible that the digital networks we invented to extend our analog lives are moving toward replacing them instead. It seems plausible that the chemistry we keep leaching into the air and water may alter us biologically. It seems probable that our attention is divided. But I also recognize the presentism that informs such common proclamations. Is the presentist belief that things are so much worse than they were before (or, if you really dig texting or modern dentistry, so much better) just a symptom of the narcissism supposedly fuelling contemporary culture? And if it is, then what to think about something irrefutably present tense, like climate change?

Thinking about writing poetry today, regardless of any answers to such queries, necessitates at least a recognition of the potentially shifting parameters of the world that will receive it (if we intend to write for anyone other than ourselves, that is). Self-awareness and honesty might be the original twin poles necessary for magnetizing the poetic globe, but how do we locate ourselves now, with so many parts of the world still on fire, so many of us still locked up, so many still rolling in gold coins? Part of the answer surely has to do with the individuation and situated knowledge necessary for using words such as *I* or *we* or *you*: who do these exclude or accuse?

Again, Adrienne Rich always seems to offer me the best answers to such questions, this time in her 1984 essay "Notes toward a Politics of Location":

> *The difficulty of saying I*—a phrase from the East German novelist Christa Wolf. But once having said it, as we realize the necessity to go further, isn't there a difficulty of saying "we"? *You cannot speak for me. I cannot speak for us.* Two thoughts: there is no liberation that only knows how to say "I"; there is no collective movement that speaks for each of us all the way through.

Like Milkman Dead rising above the last page of *Song of Solomon* or the slices performed at the end of "Ode to the Onion," these lines provoke the necessary breakage that locates me in the world, now. They both limit and open who is included in saying *I* or *we* or *you*. They tell us, thirty-five years after they're written, what poetic truth can offer: a way to locate ourselves—in history, in culture, in geography, in our own bodies, in our own time—that's not necessarily the present or the past or the future, but more what I'd tentatively like to call the future accidental. I mean for this phrase, *the future accidental*, to function as both a categorical label (the nature of the dynamic I'm sketching) and as a verb tense (the grammatical mode within which that dynamic is expressed).

Used as both label and verb tense, the term implies at least two primary thoughts. First, it implies the obvious idea of chance (minus all notions of astrological destiny, I admit): the textual "accident" that might place a certain book or poem in your life at a certain time, a placement that fuses two types of present tense in the moment of reception—the now of the writer's act of writing and the now of the reader's act of reading. That this action is always new signals the complete cycle, wherein the latent newness of what's recorded is only developed in the newness of reception—so a poem's future comprises both its past circulation and recording and, simultaneously, the eventual newness of our eyes on its lines. Second, the term implies "accidental" in the musical sense, wherein the flats, sharps, and naturals that occur when playing or listening to music signal moments within a system that don't quite obey that system's most common expectations, moments that obscure or shift the expected notes in any declared scale, signalling that what's happening, at any given moment, sometimes concerns the pauses or exclusions between expected notes. Thus, I mean "accidental" to signal the minor notes within and against recognizably major systems, notes that demarcate what doesn't quite fit into normalcy or reason. That quiet refutation of system, recorded in the poem, left dormant in the shelved book, is made new each

time it's activated by a reader who's awake, who also activates their own accidentals.

What's new in the future accidental—since it marks not just newness but renewal, reinvention, translation—is always new. What's novel is terminal. While the way forward often requires a consideration of the way back—the conditions that continue to form and inform us—what seems more essential in the future accidental is perhaps the way *inward*, where we might best understand ourselves by being humble, locating our moments as functionally similar to those that come before us, yet urgently individual, privately revolutionary, and particular. Our own present tense is not wider, faster, more complex, more urgent than any other one we've seen. But it's helpful to admit that what I see as new—as now—still remains more immediate to me, here, at the table we're sharing, than the ways I might look into other mirrors, or atlases, or histories; that sense of the new as now is what we have between us.

Two thoughts, then, might make some sense here: the first is from Jeanette Winterson's wondrous first novel, *Oranges Are Not the Only Fruit*; the second appears in her equally magical book *Sexing the Cherry*, a statement that is part of a list of widely accepted "Lies":

1. "But not all dark places need light, I have to remember that."
2. Lie: "The difference between the past and the future is that one has happened while the other has not."

I still think, despite the education I've been lucky enough to get, that I—and perhaps many of us?—

remain addicted to the simplicities of binary thinking, of this versus that, too happy to solve half empty with half full, especially since simplistically looking on the bright side so often causes blindness rather than clarity. A partial answer to what's new might involve, therefore, not an either/or but a both/and, a recognition of simultaneity. The danger, there, is replacing binary thinking with a new sort of fundamentalism, a new way to finalize and answer questions that might be more valuable as provocations or organizing principles than as multiple-choice queries. We can't solve binary thinking by simply disallowing binary thinking, in other words—such a solution would be a double negative. Darkness and light, then, might have to coexist; past and future may always involve each other. Or, as Michel-Rolph Trouillot puts it in *Silencing the Past*, "Time here is not mere chronological continuity. It is the range of disjointed moments, practices, and symbols that thread the historical relations between events and narrative."

Maybe this is why, when considering what's new, I sometimes imagine a certain kind of nineteenth-century life. In the space of one lifetime, electric light was invented and flooded city streets and buildings, photography was created and became commonplace, certain forms of legal slavery were made officially illegal, and cables were placed in the Atlantic to carry signals that used to require a three-week packet-ship crossing. But have the primary structures that inspired good old Ned Ludd to smash his 1770s stocking frames really shifted in what we tend to call "our time"? Does the swiftness of contemporary brutality or the extraction of limited resources that currently fuel our Western privileges—coltan now, not ivory—constitute any real, systemic, distributive change from the economies that precede this one? If anything has become new in our own time, perhaps it's the details of the design, not the drawing table itself. So how can we best think about the present, unprecedented portability and ubiquity of the trends that locate us after the end of that imagined nineteenth-century life?

Here's a possible answer: my friend's palm, still under the table, still flat. Here's my beer glass, already empty. Here's the sun, just so, finding all the things we've shared here, now, new, between us. And even that newness isn't new; even this now has its own exacting histories.

It's only in such moments of clear sight—like reading or writing what feels like the right lines so that my body overtakes my mind and the whole Cartesian balancing act fuses into a singular, non-binary vision fuelled by shared language—that I'm able both to detect the monsters we're always sketching at the edges of our own little oceans and to navigate past the shore into the already inhabited mainland, hair standing on end. That's not news. It's now. And now can happen any time. B

Homesick for Sadness

JENNY ERPENBECK

Translated from the German by Kurt Beals

So what was I doing the night the wall fell?

    I spent that evening with friends, just a few blocks from the spot where world history was being made, and then: I slept. I literally slept through that moment of world history, and while I was asleep, the pot wasn't just being stirred, it was being knocked over and smashed to bits. The next morning I learned: We didn't even need pots anymore.

In the society that I had been born into, the most radical critics of the government had outdone the government itself in hoping. So I had learned to hope—to live with the provisional status of things, to know better, and to wait. But what now? Now the people who had gotten it wrong weren't just being replaced, they were being written off completely. And those who had known better were suddenly left sitting in an empty theatre. There was suddenly a lot of talk of *freedom*, but I couldn't make much of this word *freedom*, which floated freely in all sorts of sentences. *Freedom* to travel? (But will we be able to afford it?) Or *freedom* of opinion? (What if no one cares about my opinion?) *Freedom* to shop? (But what happens when we're finished shopping?) *Freedom* wasn't given freely, it came at a price, and the price was my entire life up to that point. The price was that everything that had been called the present until then was now called the past. Our everyday lives weren't everyday lives anymore, they were an adventure that we had survived, our customs were suddenly an attraction. In the course of just a few weeks, what had been self-evident ceased to be self-evident. A door that opens only once a century had opened, but now the century was also gone forever. From that moment on, my childhood belonged in a museum.

Recently, I opened the newspaper to find an obituary for my elementary school.

Yes, really. Former students had placed a memorial in the newspaper for the building where I had attended school for eight years of my childhood. "Today we quietly mourn the demolition of our school." But these students, who are all adults now, didn't just use the unusually long obituary to express their grief, they also wrote about their everyday lives at and with the school, which was built in 1973–1974 in the valley between the East Berlin high-rises in Leipziger Strasse and the Springer high-rise in West Berlin—it was a standard, boxy, modern building that later served as a high school for about ten years after reunification before being abandoned, and then it stood empty for another ten years, gradually becoming overgrown with trees, bushes, and weeds. A silent place, maybe one square kilometre including the athletic field, right around the corner from the hustle and bustle of Checkpoint Charlie, an international tourist attraction for anyone who wants to know what the wall felt like. And just a fifteen-minute walk from Potsdamer Platz, with its glass palaces.

Where else could something like that be found in a Western capital, an abandoned lot right in the middle of the city, a barren piece of earth, a dead remnant of the everyday life of another era? Ground Zero in New York was transformed into a construction site as soon as the wreckage had been hauled away, and at the edge of the construction site a museum was built to commemorate those who had died in the World Trade Center attack. But no one had died in our school. There hadn't been a war or an act of terror, thank god. Once the authorities had abandoned our school, the site represented nothing more than a new society's impatience for an empty lot in a prime location.

When I go to see the rubble heap today, only a small piece of the rear stairwell is still intact. That was the stairwell that led to the science classrooms when I was a student there. At recess, the boys from my class would stand in the niche between this stairwell and the wall of the actual school building, forming a tight circle with their backs to everyone else, so that they could smoke in secret. When one of them became *my boyfriend*, that made me the first girl who got to stand there at recess and turn my back to everyone else.

What actually happens to the curvature of space-time when a wall collapses, when the ceiling crashes to the floor?

Places always disappear in two stages, this becomes clear to me for the first time when I notice something beside the large rubble heap, a droopy mountain of red rubber mats that used to cover the athletic field. The first stage: the place is emptied out, grown over—it collapses, but it's still there—and then the second: the place is wiped away, and something else moves in. Only after it has been wiped away, cleared off, disposed of, can the place that was once there give way to something else.

That derelict fermata in the midst of Berlin Mitte had at least been a sort of placeholder all that time for my memories of the school, although certainly it wasn't always a happy place, schools seldom are. A wilderness right in the centre of the up-and-coming neighbourhood of Mitte, this single square kilometre was also something like a bygone era that sticks in the throat of the new one until it can finally be spit out.

Only when the surface has been smoothed out, when all visible traces have been removed, do this forgotten place and the forgotten time contained within it proceed down their final path, becoming a purely mental state, if you will, from then on they will no longer exist anywhere except in the convolutions of my brain and the convolutions of certain other brains; each will find its final refuge in one memory or another.

Outside the school's main entrance, there was a plaza big enough for all of the students to assemble in a square formation for the flag ceremony. We also gathered there when the administration held a fire drill. And from April or May on we would play a game there according to our own strict rules, jumping over elastic bands that were tied together and stretched between two girls' legs. We used waistband elastic, and back then we called the game Gummihopse. Today most Germans would probably say Gummitwist, in America they call it Chinese jump rope. For the first round, the bands would be at ankle height; for the second round at the knees; for the third round at the hips. The jumps that allowed you to move your two feet separately were always easier than those that required you to hop over one of the bands with both

feet together. The school's front steps, which led from this plaza of games, flag-raisings, and fire drills to the main entrance, also served as the backdrop for our annual class photos, with the taller students arrayed on the steps behind the shorter ones, as in a choir.

A plaza that's just the right size for all of the students to assemble in a square formation for the flag ceremony ("Where's my blue pleated skirt? Where's my cap? Why isn't it staying on?" "Come here, I'll fasten it with a bobby pin!" "No, that hurts!"), a plaza like that is covered in slabs of cement, and when a plaza like that is covered in slabs of cement, then it's a good place for jumping over an elastic band stretched between two girls' legs. A flag-raising can be a routine, and so can a game that girls play when the weather is finally warm enough to wear knee socks.

There, on the spot where that plaza used to be, the students are all gone now, and the word *flag-raising* is a term that has served its purpose, a rubble word. There, on that spot that was left empty to make room for the students' orderly assemblies, pieces of concrete from the demolished building have now piled up, one on top of the other. This mountain of concrete has a special significance to me, because on one of those pieces I can see the small blue tiles that covered the girls' bathroom. Did I like that bathroom? Is it even possible to like a school bathroom? Don't I look forward to the future? To the apartments or offices with great natural light that will soon take the place of this former socialist school bathroom? To granite, stainless steel, oak, in place of the classroom bulletin boards bearing slogans like "The Fire Started with a Spark!" To elevators with doors that softly close, in place of the open air where students responded to the command "For peace and socialism—be prepared!" with a snappy or weary "Always prepared!"

No, strangely enough it has nothing to do with the question of whether the past that is now being replaced was pleasant or unpleasant, good or evil, honest or dishonest. It was simply time, time that really did pass in this way that I knew and that was preserved in those rooms. Time that was once the present, a shared present that included my own personal present. Time that entailed a particular concept of the future that I knew well, even if that future itself remained a very distant one. "The future isn't what it used to be," Karl Valentin said it well. By now I know what became of the bright future that our school was preparing us for. The hard slog—what Brecht called the "struggles of the plain," in contrast to the "struggles of the mountain." That plain proved to be too wide. But what now? Now there's another future. Or do the present and the future now merge together forever? And when these ruins are cleared away once and for all, will the past be written off once and for all too? Are we arriving, now and forever, in an era that claims validity for all time?

Now that the school basement, which was sometimes used as a vaccination clinic, and the cafeteria, which still served dishes like *blood sausage with sauerkraut*, and the auditorium, where our pictures from art class hung, have been reduced to rubble, I see that the two stages of disappearance mentioned above correspond to two stages of grief for me. As the building slowly decayed, I initially grieved for those specific places: the vaccination clinic, the cafeteria, the auditorium. Not for the rooms themselves, of course, but for

those rooms as the setting for my everyday childhood experiences, a setting that was slowly rotting away— as if that everyday life, so far in the past, could also grow old and weak in retrospect.

But as this rubble is wiped away, I begin to experience a more fundamental sort of grief that transcends my own biography: grief for the disappearance of a place that was such a visible injury, for the disappearance of sick or disturbed things or spaces, which offer proof that the present can't *make its peace* with everything, an apt expression. In this second stage, the *cleansing* stage, I grieve for the disappearance of unfinished or broken things as such, of those things that had visibly refused until now to be incorporated into the whole, the disappearance of the dirt, if you will. In places where grass *just grows*, where trash piles up, human order is put into perspective. And considering that every one of us is mortal, it is never a bad thing to bear that perspective in mind.

Where the socialist architects wanted to keep the evil spirits out, there wasn't enough concrete, thank god, or at least it cracked. And they couldn't do everything at once. Spare parts were hard to come by. And besides: Who owned the *property of the people*, anyway? Who was responsible for it? When I was a child, everything I saw in this city was also a reminder that the present of that socialist experiment was not so far removed from the presence of war. The unfinished present and the vision of a bright future, the destroyed past and the construction sites where the new world was being built, still existed side by side, you could see them any time. "Resurrected from the ruins, faces toward the future turned": that was

the first line of the East German national anthem, and you couldn't have one without the other, the future without the ruins. And after all, children first begin to learn from the things that are *there,* they learn by seeing what's *there*, what exists side by side in that moment. Stories only come later, individual experiences. For children, the ruins of bygone eras that ended before they were born aren't initially places of mourning, any more than hospitals are places of mourning for children who have never seen anyone close to them suffer there, or cemeteries, when they have never buried a friend, a grandmother, a grandfather, a father or mother. Ruins aren't even places of fear for children, because they lack the experience that would inspire that fear. My own love of dirt, let's just call it that, of unfinished things and ruins, was an unburdened love when I was a child, and what I learned, I learned thanks to the simple presence of such damaged places and spaces, their mere existence, the fact that I shared the days of my life with them.

Ruins were an everyday sight in my childhood, those very ruins that had cost me nothing, that belonged to the reality into which I had been born. Didn't I have my first rendezvous with the high-school boyfriend I mentioned earlier in the ruins of the Deutscher Dom, between weeds and jagged blocks of stone? Hadn't I climbed the strong branches of a birch tree, which reached all the way up to the second floor, to enter the ruins of the New Museum, to enter the one half of a hallway that still remained intact, to see the statues that no one else knew were there? Those statues that were conceived as torsos from the start, but had suffered additional injuries in a war in which they had no stake? Hadn't my father always told the same story as we drove past Alexanderplatz in our Trabant, pointing to the construction fence across from Berlin's town hall and recalling the mummified bodies from the Biedermeier era that he had seen there as a student, in the catacombs that had survived the war beneath St. Nicholas's Church, bodies that probably still lay there under the rubble of that bombed-out quarter? I knew the bullet holes that pocked the bases of Humboldt University, of the state library, and of all the other major buildings in Mitte, I always knew what it looks like when a tree grows out of a rain gutter, knew what it's like to look out a window onto an air-raid shelter, and knew the washed-out colours on a brick wall that remains when the rest of the house has been destroyed, showing where the bathroom, the kitchen, the pantry used to be. Steel girders. Charred beams. Walls with nothing behind them. Rooms where the rain falls on dead pigeons because there isn't a roof overhead. Fire walls that make pretty silhouettes at sunset. Cordoned-off areas. Empty spaces and dead ends right in the centre of Berlin Mitte.

As a child I loved the ruins. They were secret places, unoccupied places where the weeds grew up to your knees, and no adults ever followed us there. Sometimes they were also dangerous places, places with pretty views, places where we could make discoveries that were ours alone. Quiet places where nothing happened, nothing but the clouds passing overhead. Places where you could look up through several floors and burned-out windows to see the sky. Places where shepherd's purse grew with heart-shaped pods that you could eat. Places that formed a landscape in the middle of the city. Only later did I understand that what seemed so familiar to my childhood eyes was actually another era, a destroyed era that sticks in the throat of the new one until it can finally be spit out. But there was one difference: It didn't cost anything for the ruins to stand there back then. Time wasn't running, time was standing still. No one talked about money. The private ownership of land had been abolished. Real estate lived up to its legal name, "immovable property"—it was simply there, unmoving.

It was probably during that time that I learned to live with unfinished things, and with the knowledge that houses built for eternity aren't really eternal. Only as an adult did I learn that when Hitler planned the major building projects for his *Thousand-Year Reich*, he intended them to be magnificent ruins even after those thousand years had come to an end. So the destroyed city of Berlin offered many opportunities to learn which parts of a dome or a department store survive, to learn that it's possible to live quite comfortably in the bottom two floors of an apartment building even when the top two floors have been bombed to rubble. And that's the sort of knowledge that you never forget. Even today, without thinking too much about it, I automatically transform all shopping malls into the ruins of shopping malls,

I see clouds of dust rising up in luxury boutiques, I imagine the glass facades of office buildings shattering and crashing to the ground, revealing the naked offices behind them where no one is working anymore. I know very well what it would be like if all of the rubber trees in the living rooms and all of the geraniums on the balconies dried up because no one was there to water them, or because the people who *were* there had more urgent tasks to attend to than watering their plants. I see fountains full of wreckage, I see streets that are no longer passable, and I wonder which pieces of furniture in my apartment might still have a piece of floor left to stand on when the rest of the apartment is no longer there. Similarly, I've always known how the people sitting across from me on the subway—children, teenagers, adults in the prime of life—would look when they're eighty years old, I've had no choice but to transform those people into their own ruins, too: into sick, wise, barren, or overripe ruins of faces and bodies, I've known what kind of decay awaits them, and I've seen it again and again in different forms. This compulsion for transformation is still with me today, as if the decay of everything in existence were simply the other half of the world, without which nothing could be imagined.

And at the same time, I myself was living right in the middle of a construction site that could only be there because nothing, or almost nothing, remained from before—but I didn't even understand what I was experiencing. And that's probably always the case: It takes us an entire lifetime to unravel the mysteries of our own lives. Layer upon layer of knowledge accumulates upon the past, revealing it anew each time as a past that we certainly lived through, but couldn't even begin to understand.

I start with my life as a schoolgirl, I grow, and the houses around our house grow too. My own conscious life begins at the same time as the socialist life of Leipziger Strasse, which today leads to Potsdamer Platz, though back then it came to an end at the wall. Today I know that a hundred years ago Leipziger Strasse was a narrow, popular, and very lively commercial thoroughfare, with tobacconists, a horse-drawn tram, houses with ornate sandstone facades, and women in pretty hats. Jewish textile factories did business in that neighbourhood until the early 1930s. But by the time I was a child, all of that was gone, and I didn't even know that anything was missing—or anyone. Today I also know that the high-rises, including the one I lived in, were very consciously conceived as propaganda instruments, a counterpart to the Springer high-rise in the West, but when I was a child I was simply thrilled when we could look down on New Year's Eve from the terrace above the twenty-third floor and see the many flashes of light below. In school, we read the time for our socialist recess from a glowing clock in the western part of the city that we could see on the other side of the wall. The fact that the building that displayed the clock also displayed the letters *B. Z.*—an advertisement for a newspaper that we didn't know—was of no interest to us. On our Sunday strolls, my parents took me down to the end of Leipziger Strasse, to the neighbourhood that abutted the wall, it was as quiet as a village there, with smooth asphalt from before the war where I could roller skate, the bus line ended there, and there was no through traffic. That was where the earth came to an end. There is nothing better for a child than to grow up at the ends of the earth.

When I was a child, one half of the city seemed like a whole to me. Even today, although I understand that the city is finally functioning again as intended, by growth and by design, my feelings disagree. For instance, I can drive along Chaussee Strasse a hundred times, from the East Berlin neighbourhood of Mitte to the West Berlin neighbourhood of Wedding—by now it's a perfectly normal street again—but every single time, a hundred times, I drive through a border crossing. The two parts have grown back together, but for me it isn't a question of growing back together; instead, it's a completely arbitrary addition, since when I was a child I never experienced the two halves of Berlin as one city. I see how the standard operations of a capitalist metropolis are moving back into the buildings on the side that I knew well, buildings that they already occupied fifty years earlier, and I understand now that these buildings always knew more than they could tell me. *Haus der Schweiz*—I had never understood what that building with a ground-floor grocery store along the socialist boulevard Unter den Linden had to do with Switzerland. But now the building belongs to the banks and insurance companies again, as it did when it was built. And yet—what I didn't learn back then with the feelings of a child I can never make up for now with the feelings of an adult. For someone like my old neighbour—who always bought his rolls at the bakery across the street before the war, until

suddenly, from one day to the next, that side of the street was in the West—just the opposite must have been the case. When he had the feelings of a child, he encountered Berlin as one city; for him, I imagine, the wall must have been a subtraction that lasted twenty-eight years.

When I was a child, I didn't differentiate between the ruins that the Second World War had left behind and the empty lots and city-planning absurdities that resulted from the construction of the wall. The buildings still painted with the words *Dairy* or *Coal Merchant* in the gothic script of the Nazi era, even though no dairy or coal shop had been there for years, were an everyday sight when I was a child growing up in the seventies, just like the subway-station entrances that had been closed off ever since the wall was built. The wind blew old paper and dry leaves to the bottom of those stairs, which no one went down for thirty years; as children in the East, we could sometimes hear the sounds of the West Berlin subways through the ventilation grates as they passed underneath the East without stopping. We knew the warm air that drifted up to us from those inaccessible air shafts, but we learned that just as the municipal dairies and coal shops could disappear forever, there were also paths beneath our feet that were not meant for us, airplanes overhead in which we would never fly, we heard the construction workers on the scaffolding in West Berlin hammering and drilling, and we knew that an entire world that seemed so close could remain inaccessible nonetheless.

But at the same time we learned—if you look at it from another perspective—that alongside the world we knew, right next to it in fact, there was a whole other world. We learned—without learning, just by being in this city and living this life—that the things within reach weren't all that there is. That there were other worlds concealed beneath the earth we walked on, and in the sky where clouds floated across both sides of the city, East and West, undisturbed. When I was a child, an empty space didn't strike me as evidence of a lack, it was a space that adults had either abandoned or forbidden, and so now, at least in my imagination, it belonged entirely to me.

I often stood by the curtains in my grandmother's living room, looking at the large building that could be seen on the other side of the wall, *over there*. It may have been a school or a barracks. In the morning, the whole building was bathed in sunlight. I liked it, and I wondered what kind of people lived or worked there. The wall, which separated me from the part of the city where that building stood, and the barricades in front of the wall, and the strip of sand where those barricades stood, which was probably mined, and the border guard patrolling right below me, were significantly less interesting to me. While my grandmother was complaining that a dust rag she'd hung out to dry on the balcony railing had blown into the border strip and been lost forever, I would keep my eye on that building. In the evening, the lights in the windows stayed on late, the same fluorescent light in every window, so they probably weren't apartments after all. An empty space is a space for questions, not for answers. And what we don't know is infinite.

My aunt, who sent me the best care packages from West Berlin, lived on Sickingen Strasse. The address was on the packing paper. Sickingen Strasse. "The

Trumpeter of Sickingen," I thought throughout my childhood, but actually the story is called "The Trumpeter of Säckingen." And the Trumpeter of Säckingen, as I understood even then, certainly couldn't be the same trumpeter I thought of when I sang the "Song of the Little Trumpeter": "Of a-a-all our comrades, there was none so kind and good, as our little trumpeter, with his merry Red Guard blood, his merry Red Guard blood." But when you're a child, it doesn't surprise you if the son of a Baroque burgher from Säckingen sings Erich Weinert's communist trumpeter's song in the inaccessible Sickingen Strasse in West Berlin. That song always moved me to tears, and so as a child I believed that Sickingen Strasse must be a beautiful street, a beautiful street in the inaccessible West, where the scents of *Ariel* detergent and *Jacobs Krönung* coffee would drift in the air, while the little trumpeter was dying his melodious hero's death.

After the wall fell I eventually went to visit my aunt, and it turned out, inevitably enough, that Sickingen Strasse wasn't beautiful and fragrant at all, but loud and dirty, and my aunt's apartment was in a modest postwar building from the 1950s—a living room, a bedroom, a kitchen, a bathroom—a dark space with low ceilings, built-in shelving, ornamental cups and saucers, a corner sofa. Peeking out from between the curtains, I saw the *Employment Office* sign on the building across the street, and saw the many sad-looking men standing in front of it, apparently waiting for the office to finally open. Even with the windows closed, I could hear the sound of the nearby expressway from inside my aunt's quiet living room. So the liberated West didn't look, didn't smell, didn't sound at all like the West had back when it was blossoming in my young mind.

From the other side, though, the unknown was probably just as great a mystery, like a vacuum that quickly fills up with stories. "How grey it was in East Berlin," said the visitors from the West who dared to set foot in the eastern part of the city. Only now can I imagine what an adventure it must have been back then, stepping into that forbidden zone after paying the price of admission by exchanging twenty-five West German marks for East German currency. Later, when I was a teenager living close to the border crossing at Friedrich Strasse, Westerners would sometimes give me the leftover twenty-mark bills that they hadn't managed to spend in the East. Those Westerners sometimes looked a bit embarrassed that they were treating me like a beggar, they looked like they didn't understand at all how the East actually worked, and they looked happy that they could return to the place they understood.

In reality, though, East Berlin probably wasn't so much greyer than the West after all, at least that's my impression now that I know the West, the only things missing in the East were the advertising posters and neon signs decorating the pockmarked walls or concealing the bombed-out lots. True, there was plaster crumbling from the walls of the buildings in Prenzlauer Berg, and there were some balconies that could no longer be used because they had fallen into disrepair. True, the front doors of the apartment buildings weren't locked, because private property wasn't important, so sometimes a drunk would piss in the entryway. Fair enough.

But what I remember most of all, grey or not, was an almost small-town sense of calm. As a child it gave me a strong impression that I was at home—in a world that was closed off, and thus completely and utterly safe. Seen from the outside, our everyday life under socialism might have seemed exotic, but we weren't a wonder or a horror to ourselves; we were the everyday world, and in that everyday world we were among ourselves. The only things that connected us as children to the so-called big wide world outside were the care packages from the West (but not everyone got those) and *international solidarity*, the worldwide struggle for the release of Luis Corvalán or Angela Davis, for example, and as children we translated those grand efforts into very manageable forms, like bake sales or recycling drives, donating all of the proceeds to the cause. My parents' furniture was in the Biedermeier style, and our money was light like play money. Political immaturity wasn't a burden, as long as you were actually a child. As a child, you love what you know. Not the things that adults enjoy. Or strangers. Just the things that you know. You are happy to know anything at all. And this happiness takes root and transforms itself into the feeling of being at home. And so, yes, I loved that ugly, supposedly grey East Berlin, forgotten by the whole world but familiar to me, which doesn't exist anymore, at least not in the part where I lived as a child.

When my son and I are in the countryside in the summer, we sometimes roam around, crawl through the gaps in crooked fences to explore abandoned sites, the former company holiday camps where workers spent their summer vacations with their families.

We open the doors of the empty bungalows—they aren't even locked—and look quietly at the carefully folded wool blankets at the foot of each bunk bed, at the curtains that someone dutifully closed before departing long, long ago, at the *Mitropa* cups that someone returned to the kitchen shelf twenty-five years ago after washing them. I look with him— while neither of us says a word—at all of those things that have remained unchanged, as if under a spell, since the last socialist vacationers spent their annual vacation here, right before their companies were *liquidated* in the early nineties, and an absence that was only supposed to last two days became an absence that lasts forever.

Now the *milk break* will last forever in the museum of my memory, I drink vanilla milk out of a small, pyramid-shaped container, the opening slowly gets softer as I drink, I think of the mechanical pencils that we unscrewed to make blowguns for spitballs, think of the notes we wrote and passed to each other, of the laughing fits that my best friend and I had in the last row, I remember how we rocked back and forth in our chairs or played with needles and buttons and erasers, hidden from view behind an open pencil case, and I clearly remember the first morning when I had to come to class with glasses perched on my nose, everyone said that I looked just like Lilo Herrmann now, the anti-fascist resistance fighter whose picture was in our textbook, who seemed dreadfully ugly to all of us back then just because she wore horn-rimmed glasses; but my most vivid memory is of the day when I stood up in the middle of class, walked across the room, and gave the boy who always teased me a slap across the face to make an impression—and he slapped me back: a form of revenge so unchivalrous that it shocked me. The red mark on my cheek was still visible at recess. Just a few days later, it seemed perfectly natural when that same boy became *my boyfriend*.

Now the place where all of that happened is flat, like a closed book, and as I stand beside it, I know: That's where I learned to read. The desert isn't the opposite of a mountain, it's just a spread-out mountain, the mountain climber Reinhold Messner once said. My very normal school days—which ultimately weren't very different from thousands of other school days—only became something noteworthy when the place where they played out was torn down, when the society that shaped that place disappeared. But everything that can't be seen there anymore lives in my head now instead, more vivid then ever. Only for a while, of course, since memories are engraved in mortal flesh, and the older I grow, the more blurred and confused those memories will become, until ultimately they are wiped away along with me, once and for all, so that in the very same place where I used to walk around in this world with my memories of all sorts of things, someone else can walk around with memories of something else. $\overline{\text{B}}$

A Conversation with Yoko Tawada

MADELEINE THIEN

Yoko Tawada was born in Tokyo and has lived in Germany since 1982. Her books have been widely celebrated in both Japan and Germany, receiving the Akutagawa Prize, the Adelbert von Chamisso Prize, the Goethe Medal, and the Kleist Prize, among many other honours. In 2018, her novel The Emissary won the National Book Award for Translated Literature.

I first began reading Tawada's work a decade ago, when I picked up a copy of Facing the Bridge and discovered a story, "The Shadow Man," which moves between two lives: that of the brilliant eighteenth-century African philosopher Anton Wilhelm Amo and of a twentieth-century Japanese exchange student, Tamao, who is studying Gotthold Ephraim Lessing (thought to have been influenced by Amo). In alternating paragraphs, Amo and Tamao move through the same German streets, permanent strangers, coexisting on a circular bridge that no one has yet built. Tawada's sensibility has a way of enclosing the impossible; she builds naturalism, or a lucid realism, out of things that cannot be.

This conversation took place in Berlin as part of public events Rawi Hage and I organized at the Freie Universität. The interview includes questions from readers and writers taking part in Double Exposures, our seminar on juxtaposed and contested histories in photography, film, and literature. My thanks to Johan Eriksson Thurn, Fleur Riskin, Weronika Gorczynska, and Fio Richter in Berlin for their contributions.

Madeleine Thien: I wanted to start by asking you to talk about the specific beauty and insight you find in the German language, and then to ask you that same question about Japanese.

Yoko Tawada: Oh! German is for me like music. Not like a beautiful melody, but something like a structure that is the base for the music. I really like Bach and Beethoven, like most every other Japanese; that music is a kind of architecture. In German, you can put yourself in your own space and make your philosophy, your thinking world.

Thien: And is that very different with the Japanese language?

Tawada: It's not easy for me to speak about the Japanese language because it's my mother tongue, and you cannot really see your mother tongue. You are in it—you are sometimes arrested in it. You are not free from it. I had some distance after I moved to Germany, but still it is my mother tongue. How is the Japanese language? I don't know. It is not logical in the way of German logic. So writing Japanese, you are free.

Thien: In her translation of your book *The Naked Eye*, Susan Bernofsky writes that you started the novel in German, moved into Japanese, then came back to German. What caused the transitions, and what was the cumulative effect of layering the two languages together?

Tawada: Before *The Naked Eye*, I wrote in German or in Japanese. Separate books. But I had the feeling that the force of one language must come near the other. I wanted to find the connection between them, so I wrote *The Naked Eye*. It was the absolute exception. I never did it before and I will never do

it again! I wrote five sentences in German and translated them into Japanese, and then continued the text in Japanese, five sentences, and then translated those into German, and so on.

Thien: Both versions were actually completed as you went?

Tawada: Yes. But it's not a good idea! Because after you finish one chapter, you read the text through and you must correct the disharmonies. You read the translated Japanese version and it's not good, so you must correct. But then you must change the German version. None of them are original. So you don't have the base, and the process has no end.

Thien: It's almost like you have two translations but no original.

Tawada: That's right. Two translations and no original. You don't know what to do.

Thien: You mentioned that you wanted to see the relationship between the two languages. Did you find what that was, that bridge between them?

Tawada: Yes. There is no historical relation between the two languages so you must make it individually. You must find it. And where can you find it? Maybe in the common human feeling toward the object and language. Or somewhere else.

Johan Eriksson Thurn: Did you tell yourself, Now it will be a German pool of words, of thoughts, from where I will take things, and now the Japanese? If something came up in Japanese, did you let yourself accept it?

Tawada: I wrote this book in both languages, and when I wrote in German I tried to stay in the German language, but still the Japanese language is always present in my German in ways I can't control.

But it *is* German. The good thing is that German is very far away from Japanese so there is no mixing. You are *here* or you are *there*. When I write Japanese, I forget German. But my Japanese is now influenced by my German. So you cannot really forget it. But *I* plan to forget it.

Fleur Riskin: The language question in *The Naked Eye* is really interesting because of all the different languages the characters in the novel speak: Vietnamese, Russian, German, French. In the beginning of the book when you write about the Russian language's case system, it was the first time I ever thought about it like that, even though I speak Russian to my parents. I was wondering if you uncovered any connections not just between German and Japanese but maybe the other languages present in the book?

Tawada: Yes. Russian belongs to the European languages like German and has very little to do with Japanese language. But Russian is also on the eastern end of Europe. In Russian, you don't say, "I have a child" but "With me there is the child." It's near to Japanese, a more eastern way of thinking. In German, you must say everything: prepositions, articles. In Russian, it's much easier, and in Japanese too. I was always thinking, Why must you say certain things in certain languages, while other languages do not need these things? Do you need it really? What does it mean, that you need it?

Maybe we can say that Russian is not only one language. It can be the Russian of the Communists, or the Russian of Dostoevsky, or the Russian of everyday life. There are many languages in one language. Maybe in Germany there are two languages—before reunification and after.

But I think we are moving not only between languages but between systems, and the systems behind the languages are more complicated to understand than the languages. For instance, we cannot immediately understand somebody for whom money means nothing. Or these days, Scandinavians cannot easily understand why, in German, so many hierarchies exist in the language and you cannot speak neutrally. In German, you must choose between du and Sie, and it is a history, it is the system of society, and through the language you have access to this system or the chance to understand something.

Thien: There's a line I really love in *The Emissary*. It's from the teacher, Yonatani. He says, "All he could teach them was how to cultivate language. He was hoping they themselves would plant, harvest, consume, and grow fat on words." And I love this idea that it's not about acquiring language, but language itself is this living thing and you're accompanying it.

Tawada: If you want to learn a foreign language, you cannot buy it. You cannot take one word after another and eat it. You cannot really touch it. But there are so many words and possibilities to make sentences. You must go into the language and see what the language does. You cannot really control the languages, which have their own programs. You have your emotions, your thinking, and what you want to say. You cannot *use* the languages to express something, but you can work together with them because they are also animals, maybe.

Thien: Sometimes they use us, I think.

Tawada: Yes, of course. And you can let yourself be used by language. You must be aware of it, so that it cannot manipulate you.

Thien: In both *The Naked Eye* and *The Emissary*, the world has been turned upside down. The world the characters came of age in—what they learned when they came of age—is not applicable anymore to their new world. It's almost like you come to the present through the future. And you and your characters meet on an equal plane, in an alien world.

Tawada: In *The Naked Eye*, the protagonist comes from a socialist system into a capitalist world, so everything is upside down. But I used this mechanism to make everything—not only this kind of conflict but everything—new. To see through the naked eye. You know, we are living in the world of post-colonialism and post-Confucianism and post-Communism: three Cs. But it's not really "post," it's not gone; there are many systems in our thinking, and we are not free from them. And because there are many systems in the world, there is always a moment in which something can happen that you never expected.

I had to use some people, or many people, whom I did not know, in this novel, *The Naked Eye*. It's not autobiographical, but I wanted to write about Confucianism, Communism, and colonialism, and so Vietnam is more suitable to this topic than Japan. I visited Japanese friends in Vietnam a few years before I began writing. When *The Naked Eye* was translated, Vietnamese readers in France wrote me their thoughts. They were confronted with the fictive people. They didn't say, "No, it's not true" or "Yes, I can identify with it." It was like the roles were new for them. They tried to go into the roles to see: does it work, is it a new idea, or is it not interesting?

Weronika Gorczynska: For me, the most striking thing is that the protagonist is so little affected by

who is in control over her life. It felt as if she was living so much in the moment that all things are overshadowed by that.

Tawada: It's a very important point of this novel. It's also my character, and it's also my understanding of what it is to be in a foreign culture and be shocked by the experience of immigration. Normally you will protest, right? You will say, "No" or "I want to." That is how people nowadays live. They know what they want and what they do not want, and they say so. But you are not anymore in this position of control. You are not the subject of your life. But it is also not tragedy. You just look and you are wondering and you don't understand. There's only the here and now that you want to understand, and the next moment. You can't make any big plans.

Thien: When your narrator makes the leap onto the train, it's a big leap. Maybe in some ways, before, women in literature, when they make a big change, it must be a leap. It's a somersault. The forces are so intense that they have to have so much propulsion to risk another life. Whereas maybe men in literature can sort of blur from one position to another, or there's more shading from self to self. I have the feeling that women, for a long time, if they wanted to make that jump, it was a deep cut. A break.

Tawada: Yes, that's right. Today my friends, my male friends, do not want to go abroad or live in Europe. If for a limited time, or if they're working for a Japanese company, then it's okay.

Thien: But your women friends do?

Tawada: Yes.

Thien: Perhaps in previous generations women knew they would most likely have to marry, so it was the expectation to leave one identity behind and take on another.

Tawada: The men, as a first son, or from a rich family, have a position in their homeland and so don't want to go abroad. Maybe the women do not have things like this to lose.

Fio Richter: I was wondering if you knew the author Libuše Moníková?

Tawada: Moníková, yes.

Richter: I was reminded of her by *The Naked Eye*. I could feel a similar thinking about language, about being a stranger or being made a stranger. She was from Czechoslovakia originally and moved to West Germany in the 1970s and then wrote her novels in German.

Tawada: Yes, I knew her. In the 1980s, when I studied in Hamburg, people like Libuše Moníková and Herta Müller were important to me. The German language is not a national language. Franz Kafka was also not German. Paul Celan was Romanian. There are people who wrote in German outside Germany, or came to Germany and used the language—and so the language opened.

And Moníková said, also from the female perspective, that it was not easy for her to write her experiences in her mother tongue, the very negative experiences. But in a foreign language she was free, and so she wrote in German, how she became a victim of the violence.

So there are many interesting things about the borders between languages. And sometimes female writers feel more strong or free in foreign languages because they are no longer in the original system in which they grew up.

Thien: I always feel with your work that playfulness with identity is itself a kind of ethics. There's a joy in continuously new ways of looking at things. I don't mean in terms of morality exactly, but for me there's something very humane in your work. There's something about the playfulness and humaneness that come together and need each other.

Tawada: To me, it's important that if you're interested in others who are not you, and this is normal for literature, you must go into it. You don't have to think, Okay, I'm a Japanese woman so I have to write only from the female Japanese perspective.

Thien: You've always felt the ability to imagine otherwise?

Tawada: Yes. In my new book the protagonist is a man from Denmark. I feel very free.   B

Two Poems

YAM GONG

Translated from the Chinese
by James Shea and Dorothy Tse

我有面頰

我有面頰
但求一吻
我有嘴唇
但求可吻

但任我的面頰
如何遷就
任我的嘴唇
如何追索

任轉動的頭
如何飛快
任它們本來
如何接近

I Have Cheeks

I have cheeks
just needing a kiss
I have lips
just needing to kiss

But no matter how
my cheeks oblige
No matter how
my lips persist

No matter how fast
my head spins round
no matter how close
they are to each other

現成物（尿兜）
給阿石

我抱起我兒子尿尿
我想發明尿兜那人多偉大
我想我的兒子長高了
定會懷念
那尿兜
那抱抱
那尿尿

抱抱
尿尿

他此刻
俯看自己
的鳥鳥
尿尿
激射
噴濺
尿兜中
尿尿
旋轉
旋沒
他當然不會想到
長高了甚麼甚麼的
所謂
懷念

Found Object (Urinal)
For Ah Shek

I lift up my son to pee
I think: How great is the person who invented the urinal!
I think: When my son gets taller
for sure he'll miss
that urinal
that lifting
that peeing

Lift me up
to pee-pee

For now he
looks down
at his wee-wee's
pee-pee
shooting
splashing
into the urinal
Pee-pee
swirling
whirling
He doesn't foresee, of course,
growing up
and so-called
reminiscing

除非
他把自己
也當作
現成物
被抱著
的雕塑
一座從遙遠遙遠
的將來
俯看
自己
鳥鳥
尿尿

的噴泉

Unless
he regards himself
as a found object
a sculpture
being
lifted up
a sculpture from
a faraway future
where he looks down
at his own
wee-wee
peeing

as a fountain

On Boredom

ERIN WUNKER

Let's imagine it is interesting to think about boredom. The particular boredom of childhood: vague, a bit listless, on the precipice of possibility. Where time is expansive and anything and nothing might pique one's curiosity, or it might not. The kind of boredom in which afternoons are eternal.

When I try to recall the boredom and aimlessness of childhood, I find mostly hazy memories hovering on the horizons of my synapses: the feeling of sun through an open window, the fug of ancient blankets spread over chairs to make a fort. Cicadas. Grass drying in the heat. June bugs hitting the screen. What is it about expansive time and summer? No school, probably. Though surely I was bored at other times, it was always summer boredom that was visceral. Underwater time. Mornings on a screened-in porch, the ancient Naugahyde glider creaking as I tap my foot. Afternoons spent swimming swimming swimming. Evenings that stretch past dinner, the hum of mosquitos thickening as the sun fades. Almost always I am alone in these memories. There is never television. There are often books, which I have finished, and the feeling of almost-sleep or near-frustration. As I enter my fortieth year, I find myself recalling these moments more and more. This is not nostalgia. It is something else. I think it has to do with time.

Now let's imagine that other kinds of boredom can be interesting. Take, for example, the boredom of "ordinary devotion" in Maggie Nelson's terms. She is borrowing from D. W. Winnicott, who maintained that if devotion was an important developmental step in the work of mothering, then a lack of devotion—the ability simply to provide care without getting too gummed up, without feeling ruined—was also crucial. So let us imagine that the ordinary devotion of care is also boring, at least in part. I think that this, too, has to do with expansive time, but here that expanse is accounted for in small acts of giving care. The time of rocking. Of holding. Of the crick in the neck that comes from falling asleep that way. Of the one-two-three-four-five count and slow breath before going, again, for the fifth time to soothe. Of remembering one's own desire to be soothed. Of toddlers' incessant questions. Of hoping for ten—just ten!—minutes alone and then attaining them and being at a loss. But also, this is about the familiar shape of a day, of a life I built. How boring this time is, how banal. And yet how risky to say so. "I am a bit restless," I admitted, in hushed tones, to an acquaintance in the early months of new motherhood. I was quieted with a look of disapproval. Then, later, I overheard a whisper: "She must have postpartum depression." Perhaps I did. Perhaps there are gradations of boredom around motherhood, and not all of them are negative. When one is interested in these creatures and their growing habits, one is devoted. When one is interested in writing about these creatures, one becomes pigeonholed as *that kind of writer*.

Or no. That's not quite it. As my writer friend says, my fear might be misplaced. She suggests that the fear might be more pernicious than just my focus on art. Perhaps, she muses, our fear—hers and mine—is of being not *that kind of writer* but *that kind of person*. Focusing on ordinary devotions and the daily

boredoms that come from giving care. Being attentive to (even chafing against) the slow. Noticing the unremarkable and the miraculously unremarked and then writing about them. That might be telling. What does it tell? I am not Jenny Offill's art monster, who gives everything to creation. In Offill's novel, *Dept. of Speculation*, the protagonist (a new mother) considers the dissolution of the possibility of becoming an art monster—one of those makers dedicated wholly to their practice—after the birth of her child. "Women almost never become art monsters," the reader is told, "because art monsters only concern themselves with art, never mundane things. Nabokov didn't even fold his own umbrella. Vera licked his stamps for him." So not an art monster. Not even Navarana Igloliorte's photographs of herself as laundry dancer, determined to make art from the dailiness of uncreative care. Just me, investing in these subjects, and in so doing becoming small like them. Transparent and molecular. This kind of boredom, this kind of time. It, too, stretches itself across the horizon of my thinking.

I find these subjects—of care, of boredom—interesting in great part because they fill my days. Or rather, have filled my days, for days do have a habit of going on and becoming softer in the rear-view. I began this thinking about boredom in the expanse of early spring when not crocuses but freezing rain gathered on the ground. I had left the city after a hard winter. I was shaken, shaking. I am used to filling every minute of my time with action and calling that meaningfulness, calling myself useful. This is a learned behaviour, and it makes me efficient in my own way. I am also used to having command of my time. As a child with no siblings, and parents who

worked long hours, especially in the summer, I built a foundation of feeling as though days are my own. What folly to think so, really. I am fascinated by my own boredom. I think about my body becoming soft under hours of nursing a newborn. How the work of sharing my time with a small creature is raw and tender and tedious. I am thinking of how time in these cases of tending and attending another is also expansive and endless, but the quality of that endlessness holds a different kind of tenor. I am thinking, also, of how boredom gets mixed up with sadness. How depression might be a public feeling, yes. An archive, certainly. And about how familiar the descent of the bell jar feels with its accompanying darkness. How familiar and how banal. Is this what

leads us to water when we are not thirsty? Why is middle age the point when so many of my favourite writers died? Have I mentioned it is my fortieth year? Oh, yes. I have.

These are midnight thoughts. Midnight thoughts are much like the midnight zone, that place in the ocean I've learned about from a children's television show: the light is different in the midnight zone. It is too deep for the surface light to reach down; creatures here have to make their own.

Schopenhauer is of little use to me on these matters.

Adorno might be.

Of Heidegger I have not much to say.

My friend found these references off-putting. This interests me. When I began thinking about boredom, or this cluster of affects I am herding beneath the umbrella of boredom, I thought only of women. Then I did a search on "writers and boredom" and those were the top three names that appeared. Of the three only Adorno's work has remained on my shelf, albeit his work on aesthetics. But perhaps that's the same thing? Besides, as another friend reminds me, there are many valences of boredom. Incarceration is boring. Detainment is boring. Illness is boring. Boring might not be the most accurate term, I concede. What is? Structural analysis, she replies. I feel chastened. It is a familiar feeling. That familiarity? Boring, frankly. I bore myself. What does one call that? Indulgence, or prescience? The therapist tells me to stop being so hard on myself. I tell myself to stop being so self-absorbed. We may both be a little right.

After the cry that wakes me out of a dream where I am trying to get somewhere and am hopelessly late yet still running. After "Mama, I need an ice cube." After "Mama, it still hurts." After "I can't sleep." After there is sleep. After these things, I am here thinking the kind of thoughts I shouldn't. Not at this time of night. Not ever, really. Why do we get on airplanes? Who can hold the tin-can-through-spaceness of it all in their mind without feeling dizzy? Why was I not better at physics? Why does the dog breathe so loudly? Have I lost feeling in the left side of my body? Is it always this hot in here? What, really, did Simone Weil mean when she said we need roots, all of us? How is it possible to endure time and not become less than we each are, not become mean in the midst of that endurance? Is it all durational performance art? Will I have time to buy milk before the gym, before the house wakes up? Will I always feel this pull of sadness at the temporality of it all, the fleetingness? Is it just that my thoughts are darkest in late March? Will I ever stop tearing up when I think of the smallness of my child's nose and the inevitability that we all disappoint one another at some point? (And then, in the revisions, will I be able to avoid changing "some point" to "again and again in a single day"?) Will I ever write again? Why did I ever care about Twitter? What is the internet but another box that, when opened by a deeply curious femme, attacks her in her wild desires toward knowledge? Did I pay the phone bill? Can I? And then: when did I last see this hour of night? August. It was August in a small town in New Brunswick. I'd sat on the bench after the musicians had packed up and my companion talked about banality. I was sober, they were not, and after they'd talked themself to a quiet place I drove home through the marsh and across the

province, and then down the narrow lane where two skunks frolicked—there's no other word for it, they *frolicked*—beside the car for a few moments as I passed them and arrived home. After all of it I was awake, as now, in the sharpest part of the night.

I am not a wakeful person. I am a *dutifully* waking person. I feel as if, should I wake early enough, I will beat the noonday demon away from the door of my heart. If I can get organized enough, prepared enough. If I can exhaust myself before dawn, then surely I will be kind.

I wake to the alarm clock I have placed under two pillows to keep from waking anyone else in the house, which is to say that I wake to the sound of my phone. Of course, the dog wakes too. I wake from dreams that are predictable. I used to wake to a pulse that rabbited in my chest. I used to wake with mainly rage and despair. Now, I wake. Dutiful. Answering a call that has been set by me the night before. There is nothing special in this waking, save for the fact that I do it for myself. The routine of it. Up. Glasses. Sports bra (too tight). Sweatshirt. Leggings. Down the stairs for coffee and milk. Out the door in the darkness of night's shoulder.

If, as Sue Goyette writes, a bear can nudge the word *mother* and sometimes find it lacking, then I can too. I can too.

But oh, it is effort, that nudging. It tires me. I bore myself in the cycles of emotion. This is not the boredom of childhood. This is something else that I call boredom to avoid calling it what it is. There's nothing to see in my early waking but sweat and effort and the mundane glory of having done work. Every day it is the same. Every day it is like it never happened. The work that happens before the house awakes is witnessed only by the dog, who, steadfast in his patience, thinks only of a walk. Of a run. Of something that is beyond what I can imagine, for who has imagined what a dog might think with the fulsome generosity that comes in the in-between hours? Someone has, of course, and I'm conflating things. Gena Rowlands is the canine narrator in the central section of Claudia Dey's staggering novel *Heartbreaker*. The dog is an expert in patience and longing. Elsewhere, Dey has written about stealing time from child care to write. I cling to her declaration—that she steals that time—and I look at the dog. Who knows what this other creature is wishing for as I pad my bare feet across the floor, feeling the grit of the sidewalk that works its way in. It is a quiet comradeship we share. Two edgy creatures, waiting for the sleepers to wake. Keeping our own councils. Wondering, perhaps, but never asking what the other needs. What company.

Bless the espresso machine, bought in a moment of desperation and foresight. Bless breakfast, laid out and waiting. Bless a clean counter and a stack of dishes in the drying rack. Bless the folded clothes and the clean bathroom. Bless the idea of a mitten box by the door. Bless the changing focus of a life of reading. Bless the patience and desire I now have for things that once made me impatient. Bless me because I still care but won't look back. Bless salt. Bless Lot's wife, never named, but bless her for looking back, wistful. I would have, too, had I been raised with less shame. Bless Deborah Levy's *The Cost of Living*. Bless this small girl in the room above me, for she shall inherit something more than my pathos. "I believe that always, or almost always, in all childhoods and in all the lives that follow them, the mother represents madness," writes Marguerite Duras. "Our mothers always remain the strangest, craziest people we've ever met."

Let's say it is a Monday morning. Of course it is a Monday. Cold, clear, sunny. Filled with frost and the fine dust of life that coats every surface when the light is just so. Never mind that I filled the two hours of nap time on Saturday with frantic and energized cleaning. There are still cobwebs (how, in late winter?) drifting from the ceiling to the wall, just out of reach, right in my sightline. Breakfast has been eaten. Hair has been brushed. So, too, teeth. All bags, packed, have been strapped to me. We could drive, I suppose, but I prefer to walk. I want to go under my own steam. What's more, I want to carry all the groceries in one trip, proving to myself and no one else that I am *capable*. I realize there are memes about just this foolishness. I feel foolish and seen when I encounter these memes. Yet I continue—with the groceries and the memes. Of course I do. So, we walk. In the cold, we walk. Through the steam hiccuping from buildings, we walk. Across the windswept Commons we walk, bitten by wind. "Uppy, Mama," and I am carrying her too. Arms aching. Mittens clenched beneath her. No slipping, not slipping. We make it to the daycare, thank god, and after clamouring to open the door, she is back in my arms (still aching), and somehow we make it up the stairs. My arms are on fire. My neck aching. We make it five minutes early, and I will in turn make my meeting. But no. The small stuffed unicorn—beloved, *ragged* with love—has fallen. Where? Where. Back down the stairs away from the stricken small face. Out the door in a mix of panic and fury. Up the hill (grumbling). Past the needle exchange, past the new hipster doughnut shop, past the plastic-free bulk store. No stuffie. Across the Commons. Nothing. All the while picturing that little face, feeling rage—why didn't you hold on?—and that thing that is below rage that is not justified. Shame? Sheepishness? Feeling both of those and more. When did they become "stuffies" anyhow? I can conjure the smell of my own stuffed animals still. The way I pushed my face into them to quiet my own crying. Their placid brown-black eyes always ready for hugs or tears or adventure. Where did they go? Packed in plastic when I came home with lice, and my mother cleaned, white-lipped with frustration, while I sat on the steps beside the bee-filled forsythia. Lost in moves between countries. Musty with childhood. D. W. Winnicott has a theory about child development and transitional objects. They are sovereign to the child herself and vital to her development. They must never change, he writes, unless directed by the child. What pathology. What privilege. I think these things as I retrace my steps, enraged. Frantic. Bored by the idiocy and power of my love. Enthralled by it. When is boredom also reverence?

Unbelievably, I find it. I find the unicorn. There, under the doorbell of the daycare I spilled out of minutes before. There, dropped within reach of a little mittened hand, reaching. That gorgeous mittened hand. I grab it. Burst in, triumphant and annoyed. Unload that triumph on the women who care for our child all day so that I might come to a quiet office and write this. Even as I am in the midst of regaling them, I am bored by the predictability of the story, of my indulgent need to tell it to them in the break-room quiet that I have interrupted. I leave, late, saturated in my own inane predictability. It is not quite nine.

Boredom, for Adorno, marks a shift in social politics. Boredom is ideology. It is the oppositional relationship that has emerged in free-market capitalism. There is nothing free about time that is unfettered with demands. There is no time that is unfettered with demands. That's not Adorno, not really. That doesn't make it less true. When I read about others' boredom, it is never unfettered. It is tied to work, and the demands it places upon us. It is gendered. It is my partner's mother, exhausted after a twelve-hour shift in emerg in a small town, wide awake in front of the television. It is waiting for the ferry in Port aux Basques (a thing I have never done). It is trying to reach your loved ones in another time zone after you've done your work. It is sitting and wondering what they are doing. It is the reaching the mind must do from here to there, held taut by *needs must* and *get it done*. It is two hours off between a swing shift. It is time unfilled and knowing, knowing that there is always something to fill it. It is knowing this and doing something else.

Depression, for Ann Cvetkovich, is something just as telling as boredom. In her meditation on depression and scholarly life, she posits the usefulness of the concept of *acedia*. Properly the affective realm of Christian monks whose work was, in great part, self-scrutiny and reflection. Sometimes this self-scrutiny went a bit off track, and a monk would experience acedia*,* which is described by the fourth-century writer John Cassian as a "weariness of the heart." While acedia has been passed over by much of cultural as well as medical writing around mental health, Cvetkovich posits that it might offer a useful location from which to think about the pervasiveness of bad feelings in the twenty-first century generally and among literary scholars particularly. Cvetkovich ultimately aligns this restless boredom of the sad soul with "political depression," which has the potential to link "emotional and political life." So perhaps my bad feelings are not markers of postpartum pathologies but something else, or something in-between.

And perhaps not.

Then there is that part of the day when I reach wits' end. It is predictable, and while it is not noon for me, when it comes scratching at the door of the rag-and-bone shop that is my heart, I answer, weary and familiar. The straw, the camel. The fathomless frustration (with who?). In summer the herons often come at this time of the evening. I know. It is

derivative to talk about birds and to apply some sort of anthropocentric meaning onto their creaturely work. Besides, the poets have been here already. After Mary Oliver, geese are done. Don McKay has, if not the last word on birds in poetic writing, then certainly many of the good words. Still, it is true: the great blue herons come here around this time in the summer, and regardless of the seasons, I feel the day shift from *get it done* to stillness. From June to October they stand for hours on the rocks just outside our front windows. They mark something. Time. Endurance. The existence of dinosaurs. They make me laugh, these birds, with their high knees and slow steps.

What are they doing? I ask almost every night. It is a predictable question. It is an unanswerable question. Still, I ask it. $\mathbb{B}$

The Writer's Process

LOUISE ERDRICH

I am just an ant with two sensitive pens stuck to my head.
It takes me days to capture a fleck of meaning.
How often it dissolves in the rain!
At other times the doings of this life
come at me before dawn
and continue in their relentless way
until night, so that the words
remain in that secret warren of passages.

I am always storing crumbs against infinity.

On a good day, moving words from chamber to chamber,
the strict repetition of my task calms me.

I may have done nothing today, it is true,
but listen to the schoolchildren scream with happiness
when let out at recess across the street.
I can hear them from my open window.
But I am also down there under their feet,
recording their thrills of freedom when the doors
are flung wide, their final hoots
when the teacher claps her hands and cries out,
Inside now! Move those words back and forth across the page!

For me, moving words is recess, freedom, but as I am an ant
my pens quiver but you cannot hear my screams of joy.

Angels

HOWARD NORMAN

Why should I be ashamed or exercise control
Mourning so dear a soul?
— Horace

"I'm human because I'm still breathing and can look out at trees, but I'm not a being because I can't get to my studio and work. *Human* but not *being*." This was a heart-rending refrain. It was also literally true that Jake seemed physically too weak to make the twenty-yard journey from house to studio. Though after we talked all night, at around 6 A.M. he finally made it out there.

My friend, the painter Jake Berthot, died of leukemia on December 30, 2014, at age seventy-five. He died at home, 107c Ricci Road, Accord, in the Catskills region of New York. When I received the phone call from Verna Gillis, whom Jake called his guardian angel—"I know this will break your heart. But I need to tell you that Jake died this afternoon. I know you were driving up tomorrow"—my first thought was I shouldn't have left. That last time we saw each other, a bleak end-of-November day, I'd arrived just before dusk. I'd brought potato-leek soup and a baguette. I walked right into his house. Its architecture perhaps more defined a cabin. Inside, an uninterrupted living space, bedroom to one side, but definitely also a working space. Haimish, the Yiddish word for homey warmth. His own drawings on the walls and on tables, a painting by Milton Resnick here, a drawing by Philip Guston there, a solid cast-iron wood stove, leather Eames reading chair, work table, bookshelves spilling over, organized clutter. How many hundreds of hours had I spent there? It was an intimate place, and no less vivid and immediate in memory now. Outside, Jake had inventively landscaped, cleared trees, planted a garden. Wood was stacked on the porch. From the front steps you could see the studio, which always seemed as big as the house, and in square footage may well have been. Both were painted grey. It all lived up to what Walter Benjamin called a "preoccupied home," in this case preoccupied by art.

Jake had dozed off sitting up on the futon sofa. It sounded like he wasn't breathing so well. His face looked a little pale, with an archipelago of splotches on his forehead, like he'd had an allergic reaction of some sort. He was wearing a dark-green flannel shirt, well-worn fleece vest, brown corduroy trousers, thick socks, ratty slippers. He'd fallen asleep with his reading glasses on; a book had fallen to the floor. The wood stove was down to ash, so I lit some kindling and set in two logs. I went out and set my overnight bag on the quilted bed of the guest room, which was under the same roof as the storage racks of paintings and the cabinet drawers full of drawings and the spacious studio itself. But as it turned out, I didn't ever unpack.

Jake woke at about 5 P.M.; seeing me he said, "I'm a human, but not a being." I went into the kitchen. "Did you bring potato-leek?" he said.

"Your wish was my command," I said. I heated up the soup and set a bowl, along with a piece of bread, on the low table in front of him; I sat in the Eames chair with my own soup and bread. He asked after my wife Jane, daughter Emma.

"You look pretty good, Jake," I said.

"I look like shit," he said, "and you look like you haven't slept in a week."

"Now that we've got the compliments all out of the way," I said. I set my bowl aside and walked over; without his standing up, embraces, kisses on the cheek. *The Collected Poems of Wallace Stevens* was on the table, *The Testing-Tree* by Stanley Kunitz, *Emily Dickinson Collected Poems*, *Adventures of the Letter I* by Louis Simpson, a volume of Emerson's essays too. He said, "I've been thinking again, maybe for the ten thousandth time, about that Emerson idea—"

I sat back in the Eames chair. "Every natural fact is a symbol of some spiritual fact."

"Yes. I'm not going to live long enough to completely understand it. But I've come to believe that's what I was trying to get to with every single tree I drew. Or painted. Trees as spiritual facts."

"Have you been reading Emerson again?"

"His essay on friendship: it's not his best. But still beautifully written."

"Complicated subject, friendship."

"Very complicated."

"Do you think *we* have a complicated friendship?"

"By all means. But the complications somehow never forestalled the friendship itself."

"Why did you say *forestalled*? That's past tense."

"I didn't mean it that way. Don't get all worked up—I'm not going to die while you're here. I'm still present tense."

"What have the past few days been for you?" I said. "You know, since we last talked on the phone."

"Well, cancer's not a barrel of laughs. Fitful sleep. Not peaceful dreams. Listen to a lot of music. My friends Verna and Roswell are my guardian angels— Ros brings his trombone down and I play drums. He's a genius jazz composer, as you know. I listen to the radio. I seem to fade in and out. Stamina yesterday was low, today's maybe a little better. It's up and down like that. But then some days, I'm so clear-headed it's almost—"

"—like nothing's wrong?"

"Well, that's the deception of the brain. But the body's more honest."

"You've had a lot of visitors—that been okay?"

"Yeah, Verna's been on top of that. Actually, I've cancelled more than half of them, maybe even more. Just not up to it. I use the time alone pretty well,

© Betty Cuningham Gallery/Estate of Jake Berthot

I think. Depends if I can concentrate on reading. I just can't feel I'm a being, you know?"

I sat next to him on the sofa. "Jake, I can easily arrange to move in here."

"I'm not afraid of dying alone, if that's what you're worried about."

"Well, it's not a matter of worry. It's a matter of *friendship*."

"I've never died before. I don't know if I'm doing this right."

"Yes, you've never died before; how am I doing as a friend with that?"

"By definition I guess we're both amateurs."

Jake was in a kind of fugue state of philosophical agitation. At long stretches he was all non sequiturs. When I said, "Do you want some tea?" he responded, "I've read a lot lately about morphine. *Good-Bye to All That* by Robert Graves, World War I stuff. There's a lot of morphine in it."

"Sure, I've read that book," I said.

"Do you think any of my shirts will fit you? I've got one I wore to the Venice Biennale."

It was like that.

We needed a subject to organize emotions. On a nearby work table was a light-brown hardcover journal; on the cover was scrawled "ANGELS." I set it on the low table in front of the sofa. "I'm going to turn on my tape recorder, here, like we talked about on the phone, okay?" I said. "Let's talk about the angels you drew."

"That might be good. Whose posterity are we recording for, anyway?"

At the moment I didn't know how to answer that.

Jake took off his vest and put on an old sweater. He leaned back against the pillows on the sofa. His grey cat was curled near the wood stove. Earlier it had been chasing a weasel that had found its way into the house.

We paged through the notebook. It was full of sketches of angels. (I am looking at it now.) Throughout were quotes from Sappho, Rumi, Issa, Adorno, Saint-John Perse, Rilke, Dickinson, Cavafy, W. S. Merwin. Jake had always been an inveterate reader of poetry. His poetry books were marked up with underlines, notes in the margins. One of my favourite things he wrote on a drawing: "I'm exasperated with Rilke; next day I'm back with Rilke." Like a diary entry about an old love-hate relationship.

Even gaunt and depleted, Jake was one of the handsomest men I'd ever seen. "A Sam Shepard type," my friend Kazumi said after seeing him at some art opening or other in New York. "Except he's got a kind of severe introspection written all over his face." That *human* and *being* stuff was so much about his studio: he just couldn't make it out there. We tried twice between 6 and 8 P.M. The first time, he collapsed back onto the sofa, said, "I'm not a *being*," and slept just for a few minutes; the second time, we got his overcoat on and made it to the door, but this didn't work. "Look, this is a particularly bad day physically." On the sofa again. More hot tea. Then we blasted Bob Dylan's *Blonde on Blonde*. "'Leopard-Skin Pill-Box Hat' always cracks me up," he said. "But doesn't the whole album bring so much back? God, it's overwhelming sometimes. A friend once told me, back in the day, he put *Blonde on Blonde* on the turntable, trying to impress his girlfriend, you

know? Turned out, she didn't want really to have anything to do with him for the rest of the night. He'd been completely replaced. She'd much rather hear what Dylan was saying, over and over. She liked his *mind*, you see. I love that he told me that. Such a great sixties moment, right?"

Sitting next to Jake, I was intensely aware of something unsettling, but I couldn't seem to stop it. While in the moment, taking in Jake's face in profile, I was experiencing a sense of elegiac anticipation—how will I feel when my friend is gone? I tried to shake this off and failed. Right then, I understood something of what haiku master Matsuo Bashō had written when, in 1689 along a mountain path in northern Japan after months of walking, he looked over at his travel companion, Sora, and thought, Which step turned us toward the next life?

There were two books of Albert Pinkham Ryder's paintings on a table. The arrival of dusk outside replicated the spectral atmosphere of some of Jake's landscape paintings, which he'd done over the past fifteen or so years. Replete with fugitive shards of white in an otherwise dark or darkening landscape, lingering ghosts of daylight. Just a splotch or faint glow here and there. For instance, the painting finished in 2001, titled *Approaching Night (for Ryder)*, with a tree on the left side of the canvas, the rest filled with a golden dusk: right there you could see Jake putting his love and knowledge of Ryder on exhibit. The crepuscular density and unease. Like so many of Ryder's, Jake's landscape paintings filled my heart with portent. Intensity of thought and beauty incarnate in the painted orchestration of these elements, all sponsored by Jake's insistent melancholy. "I like to think that making those landscape paintings was the transforming of melancholy into paint, in a way," he'd said a decade earlier. "Though that's not it entirely. It's never just one thing."

The cat jumped up and settled on Jake's lap. "What's that line you love so much," Jake said, "from the guy who wrote 'Rashōmon'?"

"Ryūnosuke Akutagawa. 'What good is intelligence if you cannot discover a useful melancholy?'"

"*Useful melancholy*. Question is, for me, *how* to put it to good use? What emotion am I supposed to have while dying? Maybe melancholy is right for that.

Melancholy needs its own parameters. You know, the size of a canvas."

He showed me a slide of a drawing. I held it up to the lamplight. It was done in ink wash and gesso on paper; its dimensions are 28½ by 20⅝ inches. It was composed in two levels of sepia and black; there are three angels, one aloft, literally sitting on a cloud, and two earthbound. One of the earthbound angels is somewhat obscured or, as Ryder put it, "enclouded" in black. Written in cursive along a divide are the opening lines of "The Death of God," a poem by Stephen Dunn: "When the news filtered to the angels, they were overwhelmed by their sudden aloneness." (In an email exchange, Stephen Dunn wrote: "By *news* I meant the death of God. The angels get that news, and a precise kind of loneliness arrives.")

"I made that drawing in 2007, I think it was," Jake said.

"It's got both figurative and abstract elements, I guess you'd say. But it's not part of the Artist Model series. Those were done between 1986 and 2006."

"What the fuck, are you being a docent? Right in my own house?" We laughed at this, but he was right, why was I imparting information about his own work?

"I don't know what got into me just now."

Smiling, he said, "You did get the dates right, though. And no, this drawing's not part of that Artist Model series. I completed that series in 2006. I was working with pretty much the same dimensions, the same medium. I'm almost never considered a figurative painter, right? I even see all these trees I've drawn as abstract in a certain way. But the truth is, I was drawing angels all along. Just not so steadily.

Even in the margins of all those letters I sent you. On legal paper."

"Yes, lots of angels in the margins. Some of those pages are heavily populated with them. How did you consider the figures of angels? What thinking went into them? I'm being an interlocutor here, Jake: don't give me a hard time about it. I'm actually curious. I want to know."

"It's like with any drawing for fifty years now. You just put it on the wall, sit in a canvas chair, gaze at what you've done, and try to think it all through. It might take days or weeks. As for angels, I figured that the theological provocations would be different for different people. I was interested in angels as *figures*, getting the lines right, the technical stuff. Some are aloft. You need to think about the space around a figure aloft."

"But looking back . . ."

"Okay, right, well, my study of the figure of angels began when I first started painting."

"It's maybe the first time we've talked about this subject."

"Let me give you an example. What comes to mind—wow, I haven't thought of this in ages. This seventeenth-century epic poem; I can't remember how I discovered it. Actually, I think it may have been from Chuck Close, in the Village. What year? The sixties. Or maybe from a poet that my first wife, Jenny, knew. I can't quite remember. This poem was written by someone named Heywood. Title was *The Hierarchie of the Blessed Angels*, but it wasn't so much the poem as the engraved plates that went with it. I close my eyes and I can still see them. I remember thinking of those angels choreographically, in a way.

Some were radically tilted, high in the air, like they couldn't hold their balance. Falling in a contorted way. Like an Egon Schiele contorted figure falling. I remember that some angels looked bored, or disinterested, but others seemed to have this look of astonishment—and a couple looked frightened. Of what? Who knows. In one of the engraved plates was an angel that had a striking resemblance—in the construction of its face—to my father. I didn't know what the hell to make of that! Let's see, what else? There's a line from some Polish poet, 'Until you lowly eaters of bread will be made into angels.' I did a couple of drawings inspired by that line. Byzantine and Medieval angels, into the Renaissance. Fra Angelico's *The Annunciation*. The classical Erotes or putto from the Italian Renaissance. I mean, I didn't question the theological assumptions behind these works. I studied them as paintings and drawings. Like any good art student must."

"Which others are you thinking about right now?"

"The Archangel Gabriel in a deacon's vestments—that Dutch masterpiece, Jan van Eyck's—I think it's titled *The Annunciation* too. That's fifteenth century. And I love so many of the Persian angels, the Prophet Muhammad's ascension, angels in Mecca. They're really beautiful works. I like Chagall's *Jacob's Dream*. I saw that in a museum in Nice. Angels all over that canvas. Giotto's crying angels. I mean, you look at the expressions on the faces of Giotto's angels in that painting—it's like the whole range of human emotion. Or maybe some emotions people no longer even have expression for. Expressions only angels could have—something like that."

"I'll put on some more tea, okay?" I said.

"Off the meds I just start talking like this. Sometimes the meds jazz me up. But sometimes off the meds I get jazzed up. I just start talking and talking— I mean, what expressions am I referring to on those angels? Expressions from a past time, expressions people forgot how to even show on their faces anymore. Early fourteenth-century expressions. But also there's that Wim Wenders movie, *Wings of Desire.* I drew a lot of angels because of that movie. Jesus, that flick really got to me."

"Let's watch it."

And so we did. I had watched it with Jake years earlier. Now I found the DVD on some shelf or other. I put more wood on the fire. We set it all up and didn't say a word for the duration of the film, which was two hours and eight minutes.

The story is set in post–Second World War Berlin. The narrator is an angel played by Bruno Ganz, whose face in that role could imply the exact moment when a thought or revelation, having worked its way up from the deepest recesses of consciousness, finally manifests itself as an expression. ("His face suddenly etched with grief and wonderment," Edward Lear wrote of someone he observed on a Moroccan veranda.) Ganz's cohort was an angel played by Otto Sander, and I see the film in part as a depiction of their friendship under the strangest of circumstances. Although the story can't be summarized in any way that does it justice, these two characters are more or less on assignment to eavesdrop on mortals and invent ways to comfort them in their quotidian distress. *Wings of Desire* is shot by cinematographer Henri Alekan, dominantly in sepia-toned black and white. At times the soundtrack feels as if it is being mumbled and hummed by Marlene Dietrich suffering the rapture of her most disconsolate hours. The screenwriters Wim Wenders and Peter Handke declared that they were influenced by Rilke's "desperate lyricism" and Homer's "angel of storytelling." At one point, the narrator falls in love with a trapeze artist, played by Solveig Dommartin, whose loneliness, especially when she is depicted aloft on a trapeze, is precisely what inspired Jake's drawing *When the News Filtered to the Angels They Were Overwhelmed by Their Sudden Aloneness.* "She's aloft, but can't seem to rise above her own terrestrial sadness," Handke wrote. Anyway, the trapeze artist is so consuming an object of desire for the narrator that he becomes mortal so he can experience all the tactile and sensory human pleasures again and hope to discover love with her. It is a romantic tragedy, a near-theological melodrama, and a kind of monochromatic symphony on screen. When it was over, Jake said, "Anyone who thinks this is all about death is crazy; it's about the nature of being alive."

"So, the Bruno Ganz angel is a *being* but not *human.* He wants to be human again."

"Yeah, and it's so goddamn heartbreaking. And so dark, but so full of surprising light too. I mean, the city seems desperate for light. Ganz and Otto Sander seem desperate for light, for it to enter them, somehow. It reminds me of—"

Jake stood up, and the cat scattered off, knocking over Jake's teacup. He started to shuffle through some books on a nearby shelf. Jake found a collection by the thirteenth-century Persian poet Rumi. He paged through—"Where is that? Where is that?"—and found what he was looking for.

He read, "The wound is the place where the light enters you." B̅

THANK YOU

TO OUR SPONSORS & DONORS

KEYSTONES: $1,001–5,000

Margaret Atwood, Michael Barnstijn & Louise MacCallum, Dr. Andreas Conradi, Robert Cove, Ron Graham, Sonja N. Koerner, Mary Lou Thomson, 333 ANON

MORTAR: $501–1,000

Anonymous, Duncan Glaholt, John Irving, Jaye Jenkins, Pamela Krasney, Kevin & Sharon Krause, Harvey Loen, Julie Mancini, Alice Munro, Jane Rule, Gerald Schwartz, Sam Solecki, Valerie Trueblood, B. G. Wiens, Posthumously for Eve B. Woods

FOUNDATION: $101–500

Angie Abdou, Diana Adams, Caroline Adderson, India Amos, Madhur Anand, Carol & Kenneth Anderson, DS Anderson, Gallery Paule Anglim, Anonymous x 10, Michel Arpin & Denise Spitzer, Houry Artinian, Anonymous in Honour of Cecily Moos, Anita Rau Badami, Nancy Baele, Marco Balestrin, Russell Banks, Linda Barclay, Mark Bartlett, Judy Fong Bates, Tamara Bernstein, Peter D. Birt, Ronna Bloom, Shirley Blumberg, Kriss Boggild, Michelle Boone, Rosalind Brackenbury, John Brotman, Colin Browne, Barbara Bucknall, Catherine Bush, Nathalie Butterfield, David & Stevie Cameron, Rosemary Cameron, Lucia Cascioli, Wilhelmina Cavan, Anne Chellas, Anita Chong, Garrell Clark, Teju Cole, Diane Conn & Mace Neufeld, Jan Conn, Kaz Connelly, Susan Cottrelle, Brad Cran, Susan Crean, C. Crockford, Joseph Curtin, Bobbi Dahlman, Susan Davidoff, Wende L. Davis, Gillian Diamond, Annie Dillard & Bob Richardson, Eric Domville, Ariel Dorfman, Ann Douglas, Rackstraw Downes, Stan Dragland, Maggie Dwyer, Gretel Ehrlich, Heather Evans, Elizabeth Farnsworth, Fish Magic Press, Stephen Flewelling, Linda Gaboriau, In Memory of Audrey Gill, Margie Gillis, Alison Gordon, Catherine Graham, Charlotte Gray, Kristine Greenaway, Ann Haney, In Memory of Jim Harrison, Robert Hass & Helm, Richard Helm, Michael Henry, Ute Hertel, Mavis Trudy Hunter, Nathan Iverson, Marni Jackson, Anthony Donald Kahn, Barbara Kelly, Anne Kennedy & Robert Mitch Kowalski, James Leslie, Ellen Levine, Tim Lilburn, Anne Malena, Ann Mandel, Bill Manhire, David Manicom, Margaret McCoy, Fiona McHugh, Jil McIntosh, Gail Miller, Isa Milman, Marja B. Moens, Bill Morrison, Daniel Walter & Muriel Murch, Pat Myers, Nereus Financial Inc., Orr, Elliott Pearl, Brian & Leanne Perry, Curt Peters, Power, Annie Proulx, puppet café, Brendan Quinn, Peggy Gale, Nancy Garruba, Tony Gatner, Bob Gibson, Barbara Gowdy, Bill & Dianne Graham, Cameron Graham, Michael Greenstein, Mark Hage, Oswald Hall, Mary-Brenda Hillman, Jody Hawley, Elizabeth Hay, Michael Himes, Jane Hirshfield, Jeffrey Hoffeld, Isabel Huggan, Jeffery, Kim Jernigan, Christopher Johnston, Bonnie Jull, Sullivan, John Klassen, Morson Koo, Myrna Kostash, Ottie Lockey, damian lopes, Kenneth Louder, Todd Mager, Ellen Matsui, Joyce McClelland, Judith McCormack, McLaren, Anne Michaels, Mary di Michele, Dr. Mary Jane David Moses, Sayaka Motonaga, Claire & Farley Mowat, M. Nowaczyk, Peter Oliva, David & Liz Ondaatje, Gregg John H. Peterson, Corwin D. Pine, James Polk, Nicholas Roberta Quinn, Cecil Rabinovitch, Rattling Books, Linda & Marshall Redhill, Dennis Reid, Martin Helmut Reis, Shane Rhodes, In Memory of Connie Rooke, Clayton Ruby, Nicholas & Cheryl Ruddock, Sandra Rutenberg, Ann Saddlemyer, Leslie Sanders, Richard Sanger, Larry Scanlan, Cynthia Scott, In Memory of Frank & Marian Scott, Ann Scowcroft, Kenneth Sherman, Carolynne Siller, Michael Silverblatt, Marie Slaight, Ali Smith, Kilby Smith-McGregor, Adam Sol, Margaret Spinak, John Sproule, Penni Stewart, Susan Swan, Jordan Timm, Earle Toppings, Aritha van Herk, Katharine Vansittart, Evelyn von Almassy, Charis Wahl, Chris Whynot, Donez Xiques, Iranee Zarb

Brick brings international voices to Canadian readers and Canadian voices to the world.

These stalwart donors help keep Brick going, issue after issue. Join them today with a donation of $50 or more to see your name permanently engraved on our Brick Wall.

We will happily accept your cheques, or you can visit BRICKMAG.COM *and click on* DONATE.

GROUNDBREAKING: $50–100

Anonymous x 4, André Alexis, Jody Aliesan, James Arthur, Nadine Bachan, Martha Baillie, Dilin Baker, Norman Barrett, Brian Bartlett, Elizabeth Benedict, Lawrence Bennett, Roger Berger, Anita Boyd, Lucy Brennan, Dennis Brown, Helen Brown, Russell Brown & Donna Bennett, In Memory of Brian Browne, Phyllis Bruce, Naomi Campbell, Pauline Carey, Claudette Cooke, Catherine Cooper, Pat Craig, Patrick Crean, Mary-Jane Dalon, Josephine Dasko, Lydia Davis, Mary Devine, Brook Dickson & Kurt Navratil, Jeramy Dodds, Beatrice Donald, Adelaide Donnelley, Keith Duggan, Rose Dymetryszyn, Hadley Dyer, Kim Echlin, Atom Egoyan, Jane Ellison, Denise Fidia, Dorothy Field, Julie Filion, Paul Fiorillo, Charles Foran, Barbara Forbes, In Memory of Brooke Forbes, Jill Frayne, Mark Fried, Paul Gagné, In Memory of Mavis Gallant, Forrest Gander & C. D. Wright, Kuldip Gill, Stuart Goddard, Ann Goldsmith, In Memory of Richard Gorman, Carolyn Gossage, Nora Gould, Eddie Grant, Peter Grant, Larry Green, Barbara Greene, Dr. Frances Hamilton, Ken Hamm, Burr Heneman, Isabel Henniger, Michael Hetherington, George Hildebrand, Sue & Colin Hitchmough, Sandra Hogan, Peter Honderich, Fanny Howe, Victoria Hughes, Laird Hunt, In Memory of Gail Hutchison, Pico Iyer, James Jacobs, Toireasa Jespersen, Milton & Marion Jewell, Dustin Johnson, Anne Katz, George Kelly, Kaylee Knecht, Barbara Klunder, Anita Lahey, Toby Langen, Carole Larsen, Suzie LeBlanc, Cecilia & Bill Lee, Dennis Lee, Marilyn M. Leister, Libby Lennie, Vivien Leong, Margot Lettner, In Memory of Norman Levine, Madeline Levine, Cecil Louis, Ken Ludlow, Norma Lundberg, Wendy MacIntyre, Kyo Maclear, Elaine MacNeill, Bill Mascioli, Reynolds Mastin, Maria & Peter Matthiessen, Sandra McCauley, Anette McConnell, Margaret McClure, Jerry McIntosh, Arvo McMillan, Philomena Meffe, Jess Merber, Claire Messud, Lynne Mijangos, Carmelo Militano, Susan Miller, Honey Moore, Lisa Moore, Wendy Moser, Peter Moss, Javaria Mughal, Mary Newberry, Karl Nilsen, In Memory of Ron Noganosh, John O'Connor, Erin O'Neil, Jacques Oulé, Sedat Pakay/Hudson Film Works, Margarita Papenbrock, Yves Papillon, Nelofer Pazira, Lorne Peterson, Claire Pfeiffer, Barbara Ponomareff, Liza Potvin, Janice Priddy, Alex Pugsley, Kevin Rabalais, Susan Reaney, Naben Ruthnum, Damian Rogers, James Salter, Maureen Scott Harris, Wiebke See, Motek Sherman, Ian Slayter, Rebecca Silver Slayter, John Bell Smithback, Karen Solie, Alan Somerset, Peter Stephens, In Memory of Barb Stimpson, Merna Summers, Alexandre & Amy Thiltges, Kathleen Thurber, Lola Tostevin, Sally Vernon, Abigail Vines, Genanne Walsh, Terence Ward, Matthew Werdegar, Edmund White, Graeme Williamson, Murray Wilson, Jane Wintemute, Regina Wischmeyer, In Memory of Leo Yerxa, Jan Zwicky

Contributors

KURT BEALS teaches in the Department of Germanic Languages and Literatures at Washington University in St. Louis. He has previously translated books by Regina Ullmann and Reiner Stach.

BRANDI BIRD is a Two-Spirit Saulteaux and Cree poet from Treaty 1 territory currently living and learning on Musqueam, Squamish, and Tsleil-Waututh land. Their poetry has been published or is forthcoming in *Poetry is Dead*, *PRISM international*, the *Puritan*, the *Fiddlehead*, and *Room* magazine. Their chapbook *I Am Still Too Much* was published with Rahila's Ghost Press in 2019.

ANNE CARSON was born in Canada and teaches ancient Greek for a living.

TEJU COLE teaches in the English department at Harvard University. His books include *Open City* and *Known and Strange Things*.

EDWIDGE DANTICAT is the author of several books, including *Breath, Eyes, Memory*; *The Farming of Bones*; *The Dew Breaker*; *Claire of the Sea Light*; and most recently, *Everything Inside*, a collection of stories.

LOUISE ERDRICH lives in Minnesota, across from a school. She is a novelist and poet and also owns Birchbark Books in Minneapolis, a bookstore with an emphasis on Native literature, history, and politics.

JENNY ERPENBECK is the author of *Aller Tage Abend* (*The End of Days*) and *Gehen, ging, gegangen* (*Go, Went, Gone*), among others. *Kein Roman* (*Not a Novel*) will be published in English in the fall of 2020.

YAM GONG is a celebrated Hong Kong poet. His most recent book is *And So Moving a Stone You Look at Festival Lights along the Street*.

LINA MERUANE is a Chilean writer and scholar teaching at New York University. Among her books in English are her novels *Seeing Red* and *Nervous System* (forthcoming from Graywolf), both translated by Megan

McDowell, as well as her non-fiction book *Viral Voyages*, translated by Andrea Rosenberg.

JOHN MCINTYRE's work has also appeared in *Brick* 89, 93, and 96. He lives in New Jersey.

HOWARD NORMAN is the author of nine novels and three memoirs. He lives in Vermont. He is working on a memoir titled *The Wound Is The Place The Light Enters You*.

MICHAEL ONDAATJE's latest book is *Warlight*. He worked for *Brick* until he was fired for unreliable typesetting.

JOE PENNEY is a journalist, photographer, and filmmaker based in New York City. He is the cofounder of the Mali-based news website Sahelien.com.

DEAN RADER has written, edited, or coedited eleven books, including *Bullets into Bells: Poets and Citizens Respond to Gun Violence*, with Brian Clements & Alexandra Teague and *Self-Portrait as Wikipedia Entry*. He is a professor at the University of San Francisco.

ANDREA ROSENBERG is a translator from Spanish and Portuguese. Her full-length translations include novels and graphic narrative by Manuel Vilas, Tomás González, Inês Pedrosa, Aura Xilonen, Juan Gómez Bárcena, Paco Roca, and Marcelo D'Salete.

JAMES SHEA is the author of two poetry collections, *The Lost Novel* and *Star in the Eye*, both from Fence Books. He teaches at Hong Kong Baptist University, where he is the associate director of the International Writers' Workshop.

KID TEO is the pen name of Y-Dang Troeung, who is assistant professor of English at the University of British Columbia. She was born on the border of Cambodia and Thailand and currently lives in Vancouver with her partner and son.

MADELEINE THIEN's most recent novel is *Do Not Say We Have Nothing*.

DOROTHY TSE is a Hong Kong fiction writer who has published three collections of short stories in Chinese. Her first collection to appear in English is *Snow and Shadow*. A cofounder of the literary magazine *Fleurs de lettres*, she teaches at Hong Kong Baptist University.

JUAN GABRIEL VÁSQUEZ is the author of *The Sound of Things Falling* and *The Shape of the Ruins*, among other novels, and of the forthcoming short-story collection *Songs for the Flames*. He has translated works by Joseph Conrad and Victor Hugo into Spanish. His work is published in thirty languages worldwide.

This fall it will be thirty years since **ELEANOR WACHTEL** launched CBC Radio's *Writers & Company*, and even longer since she first appeared in *Brick*. She's also host and moderator of TIFF's Books on Film series, now in its tenth season. Five selections of her conversations have been published, most recently *The Best of Writers & Company*.

ROB WINGER is the author of *Muybridge's Horse* and three other books of poetry, including *It Doesn't Matter What We Meant*, which is forthcoming from McClelland & Stewart in 2021. He lives in the hills northeast of Toronto, where he teaches at Trent University.

ERIN WUNKER lives, works, and teaches in K'jipuktuk (Halifax, Nova Scotia). She is the author of *Notes from a Feminist Killjoy: Essays on Everyday Life.*

JAN ZWICKY's most recent books are *The Experience of Meaning* and, with coauthor Robert Bringhurst, *Learning to Die: Wisdom in the Age of Climate Crisis.*

Credits

The quote on our spine is from Louise Erdrich's "The Writer's Process" in this issue.

Page 5: Watercolour © Michael Winter.

Page 7: Excerpt from "Lava Cameo" reprinted from *Object Lessons: The Life of the Woman and the Poet in Our Time* by Eavan Boland © 1995, 1996 by Eavan Boland. Used with permission of the publisher, W. W. Norton & Company Inc. All rights reserved.

Pages 8–10: *Shield of Achilles*, *The Fire that Consumes All Before it*, and *Ilians in Battle*, from the series *Fifty Days at Iliam* (1978), appear courtesy of the Cy Twombly Foundation.

Page 15: Illustration from *The Grammar of Ornament* by Owen Jones, courtesy of Rawpixel Ltd.

Page 19: Photograph © 2019 Allison LaSorda.

Pages 27–46: Photographs © Joe Penney.

Page 47: The quoted passage from Leoluca Orlando is from an unpublished interview Joe Penney did with Orlando in Palermo in early 2020.

Pages 49, 80 & 83: Photographs © Jacques Oulé.

Page 54: Illustration © 2020 Lauren Tamaki.

Page 55: Special thanks to Rina Fraticelli, director of the Socrates Project, and to freelance producer Susan Feldman. A version of this conversation was broadcast on *Writers & Company* on CBC Radio One in 2020.

Page 70: In his piece, Michael Ondaatje quotes from "The Site of Memory" in *Inventing the Truth: The Art and Craft of Memoir* (New York: Houghton Mifflin, 1995); "Rootedness: The Ancestor as Foundation" in *What Moves at the Margin: Selected Nonfiction* (Jackson: University Press of Mississippi, 2008); *Toni Morrison: Conversations* (Jackson: University Press of Mississippi, 2008); and *The Source of Self-Regard: Selected Essays, Speeches, and Meditations* (New York: Knopf, 2019). Excerpt from *Jazz* by Toni Morrison, copyright © 1992 by Toni Morrison. Used by permission of Alfred A. Knopf, an imprint of the Knopf Doubleday Publishing Group, a division of Penguin Random House LLC. All rights reserved. Permission courtesy of the Toni Morrison Estate c/o ICM Partners. Ondaatje's piece will also be appearing in the anthology *The Gifts of Reading*, out with Weidenfeld & Nicolson in September 2020.

Page 72: In her piece, Edwidge Danticat quotes from *Tar Baby* (New York: Knopf, 1981); *The Bluest Eye* (New York: Holt McDougal, 1970); *Beloved* (New York:

Knopf, 1987); *Song of Solomon* (New York: Knopf, 1977); and *Sula* (New York: Knopf, 1973).

Pages 72–73: Photo of Toni Morrison © 1974 Jill Krementz. Morrison was photographed February 13, 1974, in her office at Random House where she worked as an editor. Her authors included Angela Davis, Gayle Jones, and Toni Cade Bambara. On the wall: photographs of her two young sons, Slade and Ford.

Page 76: Juan Gabriel Vásquez originally presented this piece in the fall of 2019 as part of the inaugural Barnard International Artists Series. The "superb book of essays" by Javier Cercas that Vásquez refers to is *The Blind Spot: An Essay on the Novel.*

Page 86: Quotations in this piece come from "Meditations in Zurich" in *Life Sentences*, ed. Thomas Avena (San Francisco: Mercury House, 1994); Andrea R. Vaucher, *Muses from Chaos and Ash* (New York: Grove Press, 1993); and Bo Huston, *Remember Me* (New York: Amethyst Press, 1991).

Page 87: Photograph © Estate of Robert Giard: *Bo Huston*, 1992, New York, NY.

Page 88: Image of *Horse and Other Stories* by Bo Huston from Amethyst Press, 1990.

Page 91: Illustration © Ken Babstock.

Page 98: This essay is excerpted from *Not a Novel: A Memoir in Pieces* by Jenny Erpenbeck, translated by Kurt Beals, forthcoming in 2020 with New Directions in the U.S. and Portobello Books in the U.K. A different translation of this piece appeared in the *Paris Review* in 2014.

Page 102: Photograph © Nadia Szilvassy.

Page 109: A portion of this interview appeared on *Literary Hub* in April 2020.

Page 122: Image courtesy of the Library of Congress.

Pages 130 & 131: *Untitled (Angels Putti)* and *When the News Filtered to the Angels They Were Overwhelmed by Their Sudden Aloneness (Angels Putti)*, 2007, courtesy of the Betty Cuningham Gallery and the Estate of Jake Berthot.

Special thanks to Anne McLean, Declan Spring, Mark Jull, Eleonora Di Erasmo, and Rick Sieber and the librarians of the Philadelphia Museum of Art.

NOTES

the PARIS REVIEW

Very early on I came to see writing as a place where truth could be gotten at, but also where the truth could be defended.

—*Rachel Cusk*
(The Art of Fiction No. 246, Spring 2020)

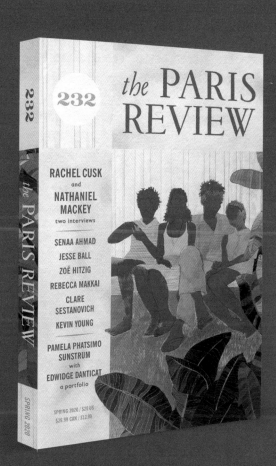

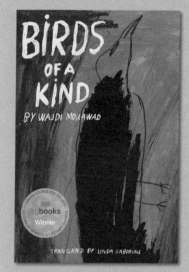

Each issue is as purposely crafted as a good novel.

— *John Irving*

Subscribe today